Canning and Preserving Food for Beginners

The Complete Guide to Water Bath and Pressure Canning, Fermenting, and Preserving Food at Home with Easy Recipes

Lydia Reed

Text Copyright©

All rights reserved. No part of this guide may be reproduced in any form without permission in writing from the publisher except in the case of brief quotations embodied in critical articles or reviews.

Legal & Disclaimer

The information contained in this book and its contents is not designed to replace or take the place of any form of medical or professional advice; and is not meant to replace the need for independent medical, financial, legal or other professional advice or services, as may be required. The content and information in this book has been provided for educational and entertainment purposes only.

The content and information contained in this book has been compiled from sources deemed reliable, and it is accurate to the best of the Author's knowledge, information and belief. However, the Author cannot guarantee its accuracy and validity and cannot be held liable for any errors and/or omissions. Further, changes are periodically made to this book as and when needed. Where appropriate and/or necessary, you must consult a professional (including but not limited to your doctor, attorney, financial advisor or such other professional advisor) before using any of the suggested remedies, techniques, or information in this book.

Upon using the contents and information contained in this book, you agree to hold harmless the Author from and against any damages, costs, and expenses, including any legal fees potentially resulting from the application of any of the information provided by this book. This disclaimer applies to any loss, damages or injury caused by the use and application, whether directly or indirectly, of any advice or information presented, whether for breach of contract, tort, negligence, personal injury, criminal intent, or under any other cause of action.

You agree to accept all risks of using the information presented inside this book.

Table of Contents

You agree that by continuing to read this book, where appropriate and/or necessary, you shall consult a professional (including but not limited to your doctor, attorney, or financial advisor or such needed) before using any of the suggested remedies, techniques, or information in this book.

Table of Contents

Introduction 8

Chapter 1: Canning Basics 14

   Canning Method 14
      Water Bath Canning 14
      Pressure Canning 15

   Foods Suitable For Pressure Canning Preservation Method 16

   Canning Equipment 16
      Pressure Canning Safety Tips 18

   Tips for Food Safety 19

Chapter 2: Water Bath Canning: Pickles 24

   1. Pickled Green Beans 24
   2. Pickled Peppers 26
   3. Pickled Beets 27
   4. Chunky Zucchini Pickles 29
   5. Pickled Brussels Sprouts 31

Chapter 3: Water Bath Canning: Jams, Jellies, and Preserves 34

   6. Strawberry Jam 34
   7. Raspberry Jam 36
   8. Blackberry Jam 37
   9. Plum Orange Jam 38
   10.   Peach Jam 40
   11.   Grape Jelly 41
   12.   Apricot Jam 42
   13.   Raspberry Peach Jam 43
   14.   Apricot Amaretto Jam 45

15. Blueberry Jam 47

Chapter 4: Water Bath Canning: Salsas and Relishes 49

16. Corn Relish 49
17. Salsa Verde 51
18. Simple Salsa 53
19. Mango Salsa 54
20. Pineapple Chipotle 55
21. Green Salsa 56
22. Zesty Salsa 57
23. Tomatillo Salsa 59
24. Corn & Cherry Tomato Salsa 61
25. Bread And Butter Pickles 63

Chapter 5: Pressure Canning: Fruits 66

26. Apple Sauce 66
27. Pears 67
28. Strawberries 68

Chapter 6: Pressure Canning: Vegetables 71

29. Glazed Carrots 71
30. Green Beans 73
31. Tomatoes 75
32. Stewed Tomatoes 76
33. Herbed Peas 78
34. Herbed Tomatoes 79
35. Asparagus 80
36. Marinated Mushrooms 81

Chapter 7: Pressure Canning: Meat, Poultry, and Seafood 84

37. Canned Chicken 84

Table of Contents

- 38. Mexican Turkey Soup 85
- 39. Fish 87
- 40. Chicken Cacciatore 89

Chapter 8: Pressure Canning: Soups, Stews 92
- 41. Cabbage Soup 92
- 42. Beef Stew 95
- 43. Potato and Leek Soup 97
- 44. Veggie Soup 98
- 45. Fennel & Carrot Soup 100
- 46. Tomato Soup 102
- 47. Chicken Soup 104

Chapter 9: Fermenting 106
- The Process of Fermentation 106

Chapter 10: Freezing 114
- Frosty Facts 115
- Packaging 119

Chapter 11: Canning and Preserving Safety Tips 122

Chapter 12: Canning Do's and Don'ts 129

Chapter 13: Some Other Food Preservation Techniques ... 133
- The Milling Technique 133
- Methods Applied 134

Chapter 14: FAQ'S On Canning & Preserving Foods 137

Conclusion 144

Table of Contents

Introduction

If you have never heard of canning before, you may be curious as to what it is, and the benefits that are associated with it. Unless you are thinking it is associated with the traditional can-can dance seen in French culture, you could probably take an educated guess as to what canning is all about.

Canning is a method used to prevent the spoiling of foods by storing them in containers, or jars, which are then sealed securely and sterilized by excessive heat over a scheduled amount of time. The reason for this simplistic yet effective system is to ensure the killing of microorganisms and deter enzymes that can often contribute to the spoilage of various food items. By adding the extra step of heating the food within the sealed container, it extracts the unwanted air and creates a vacuum-like seal to protect it from outside contaminants. Both uncooked food and cooked foods can be considered for canning.

Introduction

There are two techniques that could be used to successfully master the art of canning: water bath canning and pressure canning. You can decide which canning style you would like to go with, depending on the nature of the food you are attempting to preserve. Choosing the right one will ensure that you are safely obtaining the results you want and that you are sealing in that fresh taste you do not want to lose.

Another thing to take into consideration is your altitude level. We will not get into a geography lesson here and now… but the importance of knowing where you are located will help you to understand the temperature at which you should boil your cans in order to effectively kill bacteria. Here is a chart to give you a better visual:

Lastly, you have to figure out the acidity of the foods you are attempting to contain. Meats, seafood, poultry, dairy products, and all vegetables are considered to be low-acidic foods. Therefore, pressure canning should be used for them. Fruits, jams, tomatoes, pickles, sauces, vinegar and condiments are considered high-acidic foods, so water bath canning should be used for them. All of these foods are at risk of attracting Clostridium Botulinum, which is a fancy scientific word for spore-forming bacteria that increases molding and can introduce unwanted diseases into the human body. It sounds terrifying, but that is why this book is here to teach you the proper steps to avoid this bacterium. Now that we have a basic overview of canning, let's move on to the specifics of the different methods.

There is no doubt that pressure canning is not the cheapest method of food preservation. There are a lot of other preservative techniques that are cheaper and require less effort compared to pressure canning. This must have made you ask yourself why you have to choose a quite costly

Introduction

and technical option over cheap and mundane ones. Pressure canning, of course, requires some specialized equipment and it demands a level of attention. However, there are more reasons you need to start pressure canning. Below are some of them.

- **Pressure Canning is not as Technical as you Imagine:** The number one reason a lot to people still avoid pressure canning method of food preservation is the technicality associated with using it. While it is true that pressure canning requires a level of expertise and attention, it is not true that you cannot use it. With the instructions in this book, you will be able to use pressure canning by yourself.

- **You get the Value of its Cost:** Every penny you spend of acquiring pressure canning equipment is worth it considering the value you will get in it. Hence, you should not count pressure canning out of your options just because of money to be used to buy the specialized equipment.

- **It Saves Money:** Having established the fact that pressure canning requires buying some specialized equipment, it is important to add that buying that equipment is a good way of saving money. First, you will not need to spend extra money buying preservative acid regularly, just as you will not need to buy a fridge or a freezer.

- **It is Reliable:** This reason alone is enough to convince you to start pressure canning. Pressure canning offers guarantee and assurance of maximum effectiveness. This means that food preserved with pressure canning cannot be spoilt for a long time.
- **It is environment-friendly:** This is another reason why you need to start pressure canning. Pressure canning does not emit poisonous gas during the steaming process, hence does no harm to the environment. You, therefore, protect the environment from further damage if you choose to start pressure canning.
- **You upgrade your Culinary Skills:** Of course, everyone wants to learn new things about different aspects of life, cooking not being am exemption to that. You might have known different ways of preserving food other than pressure canning but that should not discourage you from adding to your skills. In fact, the fact that you know how to preserve food using other techniques is the more reason you need to start pressure canning.

How Does Pressure Canning Work?

Pressure canning uses steam pressure to heat canned food, raising its temperature above the normal cooking temperature level. It is important to note that pressure canning works for both low-acid and

Introduction

high-acid foods by alternating their pH level so that the foods remain fresh and healthy. When used to process low-acid foods, the ideal temperature level is 240°F since the foods involved do not have the natural acidity level required to prevent spoilage on their own. What pressures canning does, in this case, is to moderate the acidity level of different ingredients of the food to point needed to preserve their taste and flavor.

This implies that pressure canning provides an alternative to adding preservative acid to food to keep it for a while. When using pressure canning, the jars are left opened and little amount of water is used for steaming. Put differently, pressure canning helps kill destructive bacteria in food through high temperature boiling to prevent premature spoilage. The secret of its effectiveness is that bacteria present in food are killed are new ones are prevented from entering by sealing the can. Meanwhile, the heat generated through boiling regulates the acidity level of the canned foods for longevity.

Introduction

Chapter 1: Canning Basics

Canning Method

There are two main methods of canning; water bath canning and pressure canning. The method you choose will generally depend on the type of food you are canning. Acidic foods work fine with the water bath canning technique. For others, such as vegetables and meats, you'll want to invest in that pressure canner so you can follow that technique. You'll want to use this technique when you're making relishes, jams, pickles, fruits, salsas, condiments, and vinegar.

Water Bath Canning

For water bath canning, you're basically placing your food in a jar, wiping down the rims, affixing the lid to the jar, boiling the jars, and then removing them when it's safe. Here are more detailed instructions for this canning method:

Canning Basics

First, make sure your jars, lids, and bands work before you use them. Don't use jars that are chipped, scratched, or compromised in any way. You don't want them to break during the canning process. Wash your jars, lids, and bands in warm water with soap, and dry them. You don't have to do any excessive sterilization. As long as they are clean, you will be fine.

Heat the jars in hot water while you prepare the food. It should not be boiling water, and you don't have to cover the jars. Simply let them rest in a pot that's half-full with hot water. This will prevent the jars from breaking when you put hot food inside them.

Prepare your recipe with whatever foods you plan to can. Remove the hot jar from the water, using a jar lifter. Fill the jars with your food, using a large spoon or a funnel. Leave at least ½ an inch of space at the top of the jar. Remove any air bubbles by pressing down on the food with a spatula or spoon.

Remove any food from the rim of the jar by wiping clean with a damp cloth. Apply the band and the lid until it is tight.

Place the jars in a large pot of water, allowing the water to completely cover the jars. Heat the water until it boils. Processing time will depend on your recipe.

When it's done, remove the jars and allow them to sit at room temperature. You'll want to leave them undisturbed for at least 12 hours.

Pressure Canning

When you want to can non-acidic foods like meats, seafood, and most vegetables, uses a pressure canner. You're following the same process, but the level of heat is far more extreme in order to protect the flavor and safety. The pressurized process removes the threat of bacteria.

Foods Suitable for Pressure Canning Preservation Method

Pressure canning can be used to preserve both high-acid foods and low-acid foods. Examples of low-acid foods are:

- Banana
- Seafood
- Dairy products
- Vegetables
- Poultry
- Etc.

Examples of high-acid foods are:

- Meat
- Grains
- Legumes
- Egg
- Fish
- Beans
- Etc.

Canning Equipment

Equipment and Instructions for Operating Pressure Canning

Canning Basics

Before diving into the instructions, let us quickly take a look at some equipment you need to begin pressure canning. The following are the basic equipment required to begin pressure canning.

- Pressure canner
- Canning jars
- Lids
- Jar lifter
- Stirrer
- Timer
- Spoon
- Mixing bowl
- Towels

Operating pressure canning requires a level of expertise and attention. And for this reason, a lot of people opt for easier alternatives which, unfortunately, cannot replace pressure canning. However, you will find operating pressure canning very easily if you follow the instructions below. Note that these operating instructions are applicable to canning all recipes of food. You should, therefore, refer back to them in addition to the specific instructions for preparing each recipe.

- Place the pressure canner on your burner.
- Insert the rack into the pressure canner.
- Pour some water into a jar and place the jar on its rack in the pressure canner.
- Then cover the canner and seal it.
- Set the burner to its highest heat level to start steaming.

- Leave the canner to steam for 10 minutes.
- Add the weight.
- Wait for the pressure gauge to signal that it has reached the expected pressure which is usually 11 lbs.
- Then, start timing.
- At this point, you will adjust the burner's heat level to the initially expected level signaled by the pressure gauge, and process for five to fifteen minutes.
- Afterwards, switch off the burner and allow the pressure canner to cool off. Ensure you wait till the pressure is vented.
- Remove the weight, open it up and fetch the jars. Then place the jars on a cooling towel carefully and leave it for 8 to 10 hours.

Pressure Canning Safety Tips

Just like all other culinary activities, pressure canning is accompanied by different risks. Hence, you need to take some precautionary measures to help you process your foods successfully and also achieve safety. Below are some of the safety tips.

- Use the right and appropriate pressure canner in terms of size and quality.
- Use only jars that are in good shape.
- Always confirm the functionality of the gauge.
- Ensure that your pressure canner's gasket is soft and pliable always.

Canning Basics

- Sanitation is important. Do not use any equipment except it is clean.
- Use endorsed recipes only.
- Do not over-heat or under-heat the canner.
- Stick to the processing time.
- Always allow your jars to cool naturally.

Tips for Food Safety

The whole purpose of preserving food, no matter the process, is to keep it safe for consumption at a later date. In keeping with this premise, the author advises adherence to all tips and warnings given throughout this book. Infections resulting from bacteria, fungus, or parasites can lead to anything from indigestion to death. These infections and their causes are never to be taken lightly.

According to the Center for Disease Control and Prevention (CDC), in the United States of America, roughly 48 million people are sickened each year by the foodborne pathogen. Of those, 128,000 are hospitalized, and 3,000 die. In 2011, the latest information released by the CDC, the most common illnesses were caused by Norovirus, Salmonella, and Campylobacter. Why do foodborne diseases and infections occur, and why are there so many today? These are reasonable questions asked by reasonable individuals and statehoods. The answers are both simple and complex.

Were you aware that Tuberculosis, Typhoid Fever, and Cholera were common foodborne illnesses less than a century ago? Today we have Hemolytic Uremic Syndrome in children (a type of acute kidney failure) caused by E. coli O157:H7. We also know that Guillain-Barre Syndrome an autoimmune disorder causing weakness in muscles can be caused by Campylobacter infection.

Easy transportation allows infectious agents to spread more quickly than in the past. Also, these microbes continue to evolve, changing their characteristics, and the symptoms of the illnesses they cause.

Unsafe production methods, environmental impacts, ecological factors, production practices, and even consumption habits all impact whether a microbe will find its way into our food supply.

Laboratory tests also continue to evolve, allowing the capability to recognize far more infection-causing organisms than ever before. Also, the impact of instantaneous world-wide communication should not be discounted.

As scary as this information may be, the best way to avoid causing illness for your family or yourself is common sense. In regards to food preservation, most foodborne illness can be avoided if you:

- Wash your hands thoroughly before handling food; ensure all tools and surfaces used are also clean.
- Rinse produce under running water, rubbing the entire surface with your clean hands. Soaps or detergents are not necessary; the friction of the hands loosens bacteria-holding dirt and grime, and running water washes it away.
- Don't allow product to soak. Use colanders or sieves for small foodstuffs, and make sure to keep layers shallow, so that all surfaces of each individual berry,

bean, or other food are rinsed as thoroughly as possible.

- Never allow fluid from raw meats to touch, even with minuscule splatters, any equipment or utensil that will come in contact with fruits or vegetables, or with the fruits or vegetables themselves.
- Sanitize everything that comes in contact with raw meat or its juices.
- When preserving any foodstuffs, always use sanitary practices.
- If sterilized containers or equipment are called for, make sure to sterilize them.
- Keep raw, cooked, processed, and unprocessed foods separate at all times.

The extra steps may seem like a lot of work requiring extra time and energy; however, when compared to the time required to recover from a foodborne illness, not to mention the cost of possible hospitalization and medication, it is a minor inconvenience at worst.

Food preservation, whether by salting, sugaring, canning, or freezing is the art of killing microbes, or at least keeping them from reproducing to toxic levels.

Refrigerating or freezing food prevents bacteria from growing, preserving them in a state of suspended animation. Unfortunately, there are at least two bacteria that can grow at refrigerator temperatures. High salt, sugar, or acid levels also keep bacteria from growing.

Only heat actually kills the microbes. A temperature above 160°F [78°C], if held for even just a few seconds, is sufficient to kill parasites, viruses, and bacteria, except for one. The bacteria Clostridium produces a heat-resistant spore that can only be killed at temperatures above boiling. Pressure canning produces the temperature necessary to kill these spores.

The toxins produced by bacteria are not all affected by heat. Therefore it is very important to preserve only good quality foodstuffs. Avoid:

- Bruised fruit
- Split peels or skins
- Evidence of insect attacks
- Nibbles by birds or animals

Make sure all foodstuffs are as fresh as possible and processed in small, manageable batches as quickly as possible. Processing on the same day as harvested, and handling in a sanitary way produces the highest quality preserved foods. Again, food safety should be your paramount concern when preserving foodstuffs for future use.

Canning Basics

Chapter 2: Water Bath Canning: Pickles

1. Pickled Green Beans

Preparation time: 20 minutes

Cooking time: 10 minutes

Servings: 4 pints

INGREDIENTS:

- 1¾ lbs. fresh green beans
- 1 tsp. cayenne pepper
- 4 garlic cloves, peeled
- 4 tsp. dill seed
- 2½ cups water
- 2½ cups white vinegar
- ¼ cup canning salt

Water Bath Canning: Pickles

DIRECTIONS:

1. Pack beans into four hot 1-pint jars to within ½-inch of the top.
2. Add dill seed, cayenne, and garlic to jars.
3. In a large saucepan, bring the vinegar, water, and salt to a boil.
4. Carefully scoop the hot liquid over beans, leaving ¼-inch space of the top. Remove air bubbles and if necessary, adjust headspace by adding hot mixture. Wipe the rims carefully. Place tops on jars and screw on bands until fingertip tight.
5. Place jars into canner with boiling water, ensuring that they are completely covered with water. Let boil for 10 minutes. Remove jars and cool.

NUTRITION: Carbohydrates 2g; Fat 0g; Protein 1g; Sodium: 83mg; Calories 9

2. Pickled Peppers

Preparation time: 20 minutes
Cooking time: 10 minutes
Servings: 4 pints
INGREDIENTS:
- 4 cups white vinegar
- 2 water cups
- 2 tablespoons sugar
- Olive oil
- 1 onion, medium diced
- 2 medium-sized carrots, medium diced
- Peppers
- Dried oregano
- Bay leaves

DIRECTIONS:
1. Mix together the vinegar, water, and sugar in a medium saucepan and heat until the mixture reaches a simmer.
2. Meanwhile, sauté the onions and carrots in olive oil until tender.
3. Using pint-sized canning jars, place approximately 1 tablespoon of the mixture in the bottom of a jar, then add the peppers (if you make 3 small incisions on each pepper, the flavors of the brine will infuse more quickly).
4. Add one bay leaf and 1/2 teaspoon of oregano to each jar. Seal the jars, and process in a hot water bath for 10 minutes.
5. The flavor for these peppers will be best after at least two weeks.

Nutrition: Carbohydrates 17.59g; Fat 1.7g; Protein 1.15g; Sodium 50mg; Calories – 140

3. Pickled Beets

Preparation time: 85 minutes

Cooking time: 35 minutes

Servings: 4 pints

INGREDIENTS:

- 3 lbs. fresh, small beets
- 2 sugar cups
- 2 water cups
- 2 cider vinegar cups
- 2 cinnamon sticks
- 1 tsp. whole cloves
- 1 tsp. whole allspice

DIRECTIONS:

1. Scrub beets and detruncate tops to 1 inch. Put in a Dutch oven and cover with water. Bring to a boil.
2. Reduce heat and let simmer, covered, until tender, 25-35 minutes.
3. Remove from water and let cool. Peel beets and cut into fourths.
4. Place beets in a Dutch oven with vinegar, sugar, and water.
5. Wrap cinnamon sticks, cloves, and allspice in a double thickness of cheesecloth. Add to beet mixture.
6. Bring to a boil, then reduce heat and cover. Let simmer 10 minutes. Discard spice bag.
7. Pack beets into four hot sterilized 1-pint jars to within ½-inch of the top.
8. Carefully scoop the hot liquid over beets, leaving ¼-inch space of the top. Remove air bubbles and if necessary, adjust headspace by adding hot mixture. Wipe the rims carefully. Place tops on jars and screw on bands until fingertip tight.
9. Place jars into canner with boiling water, ensuring that they are completely covered with water. Let boil for 35 minutes. Remove jars and cool.

NUTRITION: Carbohydrates 12g; Fat 0g; Protein 1g; Sodium 44mg; Calories 53

4. Chunky Zucchini Pickles

Preparation time: 85 minutes

Cooking time: 35 minutes

Servings: 4 pints

INGREDIENTS:

- 14 cups seeded, unpeeled zucchini (I peeled half of them because this zucchini was huge and the skin was tougher than smaller zucchini)
- 6 cups finely chopped onions
- 1/4 cup pickling or canning salt
- 3 cups granulated sugar
- 4 tbsp. Clearjel (I have never seen this in stores but you can purchase it online ~ I used 2 tbsp. of corn starch)
- 1/4 cup dry mustard
- 1 tbsp. ground ginger
- 1 tsp. ground turmeric
- 1/2 cup water
- 2 cups white vinegar
- 1 red bell pepper, seeded and finely chopped

DIRECTIONS:

1. In a large glass or stainless steel bowl, combine zucchini and onions. Sprinkle with pickling salt, cover, and let stand at room temperature for 1 hour. Transfer to a colander placed over a sink and drain thoroughly. Note: I also rinsed half the mixture

because that is what I've done in the past with pickles...but it says DRAIN not rinse. They still seemed salty.
2. Prepare for water-bath canning. Sterilize jars in the oven on 250F for 30 minutes.
3. In a large stainless steel saucepan, combine sugar, Clearjel or corn starch, mustard, ginger, and turmeric. Stir dry ingredients well. Gradually blend in water. Add vinegar and red pepper.
4. Bring to a boil over medium-high heat, stirring frequently to dissolve sugar and prevent lumps from forming. Reduce heat and boil gently, stirring frequently, until mixture thickens about 5 minutes. Add drained zucchini mixture and return to a boil.
5. Ladle hot zucchini mixture into hot sterilized jars, leaving 1/2" headspace. Remove air bubbles and adjust headspace, if necessary, by adding more hot zucchini mixture. Wipe rim with a damp paper towel. Place snaps and rings on each jar, screwing bands down until they are fingertip-tight.
6. Place jars in canner, ensuring they are completely covered with water. Bring to a full rolling boil and process for 10 minutes. When time is up, turn off the heat, remove canner lid and wait 5 minutes before removing jars to a folded towel on the counter.
7. Check seals, label, and store. Refrigerate any unsealed jars.

NUTRITION: Carbohydrates 154.14g; Fat 3.47g; Protein 11.58g; Sodium 395mg; Calories 683

5. Pickled Brussels Sprouts

Preparation time: 30 minutes

Cooking time: 10 minutes

Servings: 6 pints

INGREDIENTS:

- 3 lbs. fresh Brussels sprouts halved
- 1 medium sweet red pepper, finely chopped
- 6 garlic cloves, halved
- 1 medium onion, thinly sliced
- 2 tsp. crushed red pepper flakes
- 1 tbsp. celery seed
- 1 tbsp. whole peppercorns
- 3 tbsp. canning salt
- ½ sugar cup

Water Bath Canning: Pickles

- 2½ white vinegar cups
- 2½ water cups

DIRECTIONS:

1. Fill a Dutch oven three-fourths full with water; bring to a boil.
2. Add Brussels sprouts in batches, cooking, uncovered, 4 minutes until tender-crisp.
3. With a slotted spoon remove and drop into ice water. Drain and pat dry.
4. Pack Brussels sprouts into six hot 1-pint jars.
5. Divide garlic and pepper flakes among jars.
6. In a large saucepan, bring remaining ingredients to a boil.
7. Carefully scoop the hot liquid over Brussels sprouts, leaving ¼-inch space of the top. Remove air bubbles and if necessary, adjust headspace by adding hot mixture. Wipe the rims carefully. Place tops on jars and screw on bands until fingertip tight.
8. Place jars into canner with simmering water, ensuring that they are completely covered with water. Let boil for 10 minutes. Remove jars and cool.

NUTRITION: Carbohydrates 3g; Fat 0g; Protein 1g; Sodium 11mg; Calories 14

Water Bath Canning: Pickles

Chapter 3: Water Bath Canning: Jams, Jellies, and Preserves

6. Strawberry Jam

Preparation time: 30 minutes

Cooking time: 10 minutes

Servings: 4 pints

INGREDIENTS:

- 2 quarts of whole strawberries
- 7 cups of sugar
- ¼ cup of lemon juice
- 3 fluid ounces of liquid pectin (1 Pouch)

Directions:

1. Remove stems and caps from strawberries.
2. Wash strawberries thoroughly but quickly.
3. Press the washed strawberries through a strainer or mash with a potato masher if preferred.
4. Measure 4 cups of strawberries (crushed) into a large kettle
5. Now add the lemon juice and sugar and stir well.
6. Now bring the kettle to a vigorous boil.
7. When kettle starts to boil vigorously, leave it on the heat for 1 minute, and keep stirring. When the minute has elapsed remove kettle from the heat.
8. Now add the pectin and stir in.

9. Using a metal spoon, you will need to skim off foam.
10. Immediately fill your jars leaving ¼ inch headspace.
11. Clean jar rims, adjust lids, and heat process.
12. Process for 5 minutes at altitudes less than 1,000 feet or 10 minutes at altitudes above 1,000 feet

NUTRITION: Carbohydrates 274.56g; Fat 0.31g; Protein 1.06g; Sodium 7mg; Calories 1063

7. Raspberry Jam

Preparation Time: 5 minutes

Cooking Time: 15 minutes

Servings: 5 half-pint jars

INGREDIENTS:
- 4 cups of raspberries
- 1 package of pectin
- 2 tablespoons of lemon juice
- 3 ½ cups of sugar

DIRECTIONS:
1. Crush the raspberries in a large saucepan, and put on high heat. Add the lemon juice and the pectin. Bring to a boil while stirring constantly.
2. Add the sugar and mix until dissolved. Let it cook for one more minute, and then remove from heat.
3. Pour the jams into the jars equally, cover, and let the jars sit in a water bath for about 10 minutes.
4. Let cool completely before storing.

NUTRITION: Carbohydrates 158.93g; Fat 0.36g; Protein 2.19g; Sodium 35mg; Calories 616

8. Blackberry Jam

Preparation Time: 5 minutes
Cooking Time: 15 minutes
Servings: 4 half-pints

INGREDIENTS:
- 4 crushed blackberries cups
- 4 sugar cups

DIRECTIONS:
1. Place the crushed blackberries into a large stockpot. Add the sugar and let rest for 1 hour. Bring to a boil over medium-high heat, stirring constantly, until the mixture thickens. Remove the pot from heat and skim.
2. Pour the mixture into sterile jars and adjust the lids. Process for 5 minutes in boiling water bath.

NUTRITION: Carbohydrates 211.87g; Fat 0.48g; Protein 4.47g; Sodium 13mg; Calories 833

9. Plum Orange Jam

Preparation time: 30 minutes

Cooking time: 5 minutes

Servings: 10 half-pints

INGREDIENTS:

- 10 cups chopped plums, skinless
- 1 cup of orange juice
- 1 package pectin
- 3 sugar cups
- 3 tbsp. grated orange zest
- 1½ tsp. ground cinnamon

DIRECTIONS:

1. In a Dutch oven, combine orange juice and plums and bring to boil.

2. Reduce heat and simmer, covered, 5-7 minutes or until softened, stirring occasionally.
3. Stir in pectin. Bring to a rolling boil, stirring constantly.
4. Stir in cinnamon, sugar, and orange zest. Let boil for 1 minute, stirring until sugar completely dissolves.
5. Remove from heat and skim off foam.
6. Scoop the hot mixture in hot sterilized half-pint jars, leaving ¼-inch space of the top. Remove air bubbles and if necessary, adjust headspace by adding hot mixture. Wipe the rims carefully. Place tops on jars and screw on bands until fingertip tight.
7. Place jars into canner with boiling water, ensuring that they are completely covered with water. Let boil for 5 minutes. Remove jars and cool.

NUTRITION: Carbohydrates 13g; Fat 0g; Protein 0g; Calories 50

10. Peach Jam

Preparation time: 30 minutes

Cooking time: 5 minutes

Servings: 8 half-pints

INGREDIENTS:

- 4 ¼ cups crushed peaches
- ¼ cup lemon juice
- 7 sugar cups
- ½ bottle liquid pectin (1.5 oz.)

DIRECTIONS:

1. Place the crushed peaches in a large pot. Add the sugar and the lemon juice and bring to a boil, stirring constantly, for 1 minute. Remove the pot from heat and stir in the pectin.
2. Pour the mixture into sterile jars and adjust the lids. Process for 5 minutes in a boiling water bath.

NUTRITION: Carbohydrates 185.1g; Fat 0.25g; Protein 1.04g; Calories 713

11. Grape Jelly

Preparation time: 30 minutes

Cooking time: 5 minutes

Servings: 4 half-pints

INGREDIENTS:

- 4 cups of prepared juice (about 3 kilos of full ripe Concord grapes)
- 7 cups (3 pounds) of sugar
- 1/2 bottle of fruit pectin

DIRECTIONS:

1. First, prepare the fruit. Root and crush about 3 kg of fully ripe grapes. Add
2. 1/2 cup of water; boil, cover for 10 minutes. Put it in the jelly cloth or bag and squeeze the juice. Measure 4 glasses in a very large pot. (If using wild grapes or other peel, use 3 1/2 cups of juice and add 1/4 cup of filtered lemon juice.)
3. To the juice measured in a pot, add the exact amount of sugar specified in the recipe. Mix well.
4. Put on high heat and boil, stirring constantly. Stir at once. Then bring it to a full boil for 1 minute, stirring constantly. Remove from the heat, filter the foam with a metal spoon, and quickly pour it into the glasses.
5. Process for 10 minutes after pouring into the sterilized jars

NUTRITION: Carbohydrates 208.37g; Fat 0.3g; Protein0.4g; Calories 820

12. Apricot Jam

Preparation Time: 15 minutes

Cooking Time: 45 minutes

Servings: 10 cups

INGREDIENTS:

- 8 cups of diced apricots, peeled and cored
- ¼ cup of lemon juice
- 6 cups of sugar

DIRECTIONS:

1. Mix all of the ingredients together in a large stock pot, and stir until the sugar is dissolved.
2. Once at a rolling boil, let it boil for about 30 minutes, then remove from heat and put into jars.
3. Let the jars sit in a water bath for about 10 minutes.
4. Let cool completely before storing.

NUTRITION: Carbohydrates 250.8g; Fat 1.9g; Protein 7.09g; Calories 971

13. Raspberry Peach Jam

Preparation time: 35 minutes

Cooking time: 15 minutes

Servings: 3 half-pints

INGREDIENTS:

- 2⅔ cups peeled, chopped peaches
- 1½ cup crushed raspberries
- 3 sugar cups
- 1½ tsp. lemon juice

DIRECTIONS:

1. In a Dutch oven, combine all ingredients.
2. Cook over medium-low heat. Stir until the sugar has dissolved and the mixture is bubbly about 10 minutes.
3. Bring to a full boil for 15 minutes, stirring constantly.

4. Remove from heat and skim off foam.
5. Carefully scoop the hot mixture into hot sterilized half-pint jars, leaving ¼-inch space of the top. Remove air bubbles. Wipe the rims carefully. Place tops on jars and screw on bands until fingertip tight.
6. Place jars into canner with boiling water, ensuring that they are completely covered with water. Let boil for 15 minutes. Remove jars and cool.

NUTRITION: Carbohydrates 8g; Fat 0g; Protein 0g; Calories 33

14. Apricot Amaretto Jam

Preparation time: 30 minutes

Cooking time: 10 minutes

Servings: 8 half-pints

INGREDIENTS:

- 4¼ cups peeled, crushed apricots
- ¼ cup lemon juice
- 6¼ cups sugar, divided
- 1 package powdered fruit pectin
- ½ teaspoon unsalted butter
- ⅓ Cup amaretto

DIRECTIONS:

1. In a Dutch oven, combine lemon juice and apricots.

2. In a small bowl, combine pectin and ¼ cup sugar. Stir into apricot mixture and add butter. Bring to a full boil over medium-high heat, stirring constantly.
3. Stir in the remaining sugar and let boil 1-2 minutes, stirring constantly.
4. Remove from heat and stir in amaretto.
5. Let the jam sit for 5 minutes, stirring occasionally.
6. Divide the hot mixture between eight hot sterilized half-pint jars, leaving ¼-inch space of the top. Wipe the rims carefully. Place tops on jars and screw on bands until fingertip tight.
7. Place jars into canner with boiling water, ensuring that they are completely covered with water. Let boil for 10 minutes. Remove jars and cool.

NUTRITION: Carbohydrates 21g; Fat 0g; Protein 0g; Calories 86

15. Blueberry Jam

Preparation Time: 20 minutes

Cooking Time: 30 minutes

Servings: 6 half-pint jars

INGREDIENTS:

- 2 pints of blueberries
- 2 tablespoons of lemon juice
- 3 ounces of pectin
- 5 ¼ cups of sugar

DIRECTIONS:

1. Combine all ingredients into a large pot and bring to a boil, stir until sugar has dissolved about 20 minutes.
2. Remove from heat and put into jars, let the jars sit in a water bath for 30 minutes.
3. Let cool completely before storing.

NUTRITION: Carbohydrates 125.6g; Fat 0.58g; Protein 1.13g; Calories 493

Chapter 4: Water Bath Canning: Salsas and Relishes

16. Corn Relish

Preparation Time: 20 minutes

Cooking Time: 50 minutes

Servings: 3-4 pints

INGREDIENTS:
- 1 large cucumber, peeled, seeded, roughly chopped
- 2 cups of chopped onions
- 1 red bell peppers, seeded and chopped
- 4 cups corn kernels (cut from 4-6 ears, depending on how big the ears are)
- 2 plum or Roma tomatoes, diced the size of a corn kernel
- 1 red or green serrano chile peppers, seeded and minced
- 1 1/4 cups sugar
- 2 tablespoons kosher salt
- 1/2 teaspoon black pepper
- 1 1/2 cups apple cider vinegar (5% acidity)

- 1/2 teaspoon turmeric
- 2 teaspoons mustard seeds
- 1/2 teaspoon ground cumin

DIRECTIONS:
1. Pulse cucumbers, onions, bell peppers: Working in batches if necessary, pulse the cucumbers, onions, and bell peppers in a food processor just 3 or 4 pulses, so they are still distinguishable from each other, not puréed.
2. Combine with remaining ingredients, simmer 25 minutes: Place mixture in a medium-sized (4 to 6-quart), thick-bottomed pot. Add the corn, tomatoes, serano chiles, sugar, salt, pepper, vinegar, turmeric, mustard seed, and ground cumin. Bring to a boil. Reduce heat to a simmer. Cover and cook for 25 minutes.
3. Scoop into jars: Spoon the corn relish into clean jars and seal, will last for 4-6 weeks refrigerated.

TIP: If you would like to store your pickles outside of the refrigerator, sterilize canning jars before canning, and process the relish-filled jars in a hot water bath for 15 minutes after canning. Review more detailed canning instructions in our recipe for bread and butter pickles.

NUTRITION: Carbohydrates 81.26g; Fat 1.98g; Protein 6.87g; Calories 354

17. Salsa Verde

Preparation Time: 20 minutes

Cooking Time: 10 minutes

Servings: 3 pints

INGREDIENTS:

- 3 glass pint jars with lids and bands
- 12 medium green tomatoes, cored, peeled and diced
- 6 to 8 jalapenos, seeded and minced
- 2 large red onions, diced
- 1 teaspoon of minced garlic
- ½ cup of fresh lime juice
- ½ cup of fresh chopped cilantro
- 1 ½ teaspoons ground cumin
- 1 teaspoon dried oregano
- Salt and pepper to taste

DIRECTIONS:

1. Prepare your water bath canner as well as your lids and bands.
2. Combine the tomatoes, jalapenos, onion, garlic, and lime juice in a large saucepan.
3. Cover and bring to a boil then stir in the remaining ingredients.
4. Reduce heat and simmer for 5 minutes then spoon the mixture into your jars, leaving about ½-inch of headspace.
5. Clean the rims add the lid and seal with a metal band then place the jars in the water bath canner and bring the water to boil.

6. Process the jars for 20 minutes then remove the jars and wipe them dry.
7. Place the jars on a canning rack and cool for 24 hours before storing it.

Nutrition: Carbohydrates 63.26g; Fat 2.27g; Protein 12.1g; Calories 276

18. Simple Salsa

Preparation Time: 20 minutes

Cooking Time: 10 minutes

Servings: 3 pints

INGREDIENTS:

- 4 cups of slicing tomatoes (peeled, cored and chopped)
- 2 cups of green chilies (seeded and chopped)
- ¾ cup of onions (chopped)
- ½ cup of jalapeno peppers (seeded and chopped)
- 4 garlic cloves (chopped finely)
- 1 teaspoon of ground cumin
- 1 tablespoon of cilantro
- 1 tablespoon of oregano
- 2 cups of distilled white vinegar
- 1 ½ teaspoon of table salt

DIRECTIONS:

1. Place all the ingredients above in a large pot. Place the pot on the stove and bring to a rolling boil while stirring constantly to prevent burning.
2. Reduce the heat a bit and let the mixture simmer for about 20 minutes. Stir frequently.
3. Divide the salsa among 4 jars. Make sure to leave about ½-inch of space at the top of each jar. Place the lids on the jars and process using the water bath canning method for 15 to 25 minutes.

NUTRITION: Carbohydrates 37.18g; Fat 9.35g; Protein 9.33g; Calories 225

19. Mango Salsa

Preparation Time: 20 minutes

Cooking Time: 10 minutes

Servings: 3 pints

INGREDIENTS:
- 1/2 water cup
- 1 ¼ cup of cider vinegar, 5%
- 2 teaspoons of ginger, chopped finely
- 1 ½ cup of red bell pepper, diced
- 1/2 teaspoon of red pepper flakes, crushed
- 6 cups of mango, unripe, diced
- 1/2 cup of yellow onion, chopped finely
- 2 teaspoons of garlic, chopped finely
- 1 cup of brown sugar, light

DIRECTIONS:
1. Thoroughly wash the mangoes and the rest of the produce.
2. Peel the mangoes before chopping in half-inch cubes.
3. Chop the yellow onion into fine bits and dice the red bell pepper in half-inch strips. Place in a stockpot or Dutch oven. Add all other ingredients, stir to combine, and heat over high heat.
4. Once the mixture is boiling, give it a good stir to dissolve the sugar. Turn the heat down to medium and allow the mixture to simmer for about five minutes.
5. Pour the hot salsa into clean and hot Mason jars, leaving half an inch of headspace in each jar. Pour the hot liquid into it to fill each jar half an inch from the rim.
6. Take out any air bubbles before securing the jar lids. Place in the pressure canner and process for ten minutes.

NUTRITION: Carbohydrates 66.93g; Fat 3.4g; Protein 2.76g; Calories 299

20. Pineapple Chipotle

Preparation Time: 20 minutes

Cooking Time: 10 minutes

Servings: 3 pints

INGREDIENTS:

- 4 Cups of seeded papaya
- 2 Cups of chopped or cubed pineapples
- 1 Cup of raisins
- 1 Cup of lemon juice
- ½ Cup of lime juice
- ½ Cup of pineapple juice
- ½ Cup of Anaheim peppers
- 2 Teaspoons of chopped onions
- 2 Teaspoons of chopped cilantro
- 2 Teaspoons of brown sugar

DIRECTIONS:

1. Add together all 10 ingredients together in a saucepan and bring to a bowl, but you need to stir constantly.
2. Reduce to a steady simmer and let thicken but still stirring constantly.
3. Add to the canning jars and seal.

NUTRITION: Carbohydrates 60.1g; Fat 0.93g; Protein 2.24g; Calories 233

21. Green Salsa

Preparation Time: 20 minutes

Cooking Time: 10 minutes

Servings: 3 pints

INGREDIENTS:

- 7 Cups of chopped green tomatoes
- 3 Cups of chopped jalapenos
- 2 Cups of chopped red onions
- 2 Teaspoons of minced garlic
- ½ Cup of lime juice
- ½ Cup of finely packed chopped cilantro
- 2 Tsp. ground cumin

DIRECTIONS:

1. Combine all the vegetables and the garlic and lime in a saucepan and boil then simmer for 5 minutes, spoon salsa into canning jars, and leave ¼" at the top for the canning process.

NUTRITION: Carbohydrates 30.31g; Fat 1.22g; Protein 5.65g; Calories 133

22. Zesty Salsa

Preparation Time: 20 minutes

Cooking Time: 10 minutes

Servings: 6 pints

INGREDIENTS:

- 10 cups roughly chopped tomatoes
- 5 cups chopped and seeded bell peppers
- 5 cups chopped onions
- 2 1/2 cups hot peppers, chopped, seeded
- 1 1/4 cups cider vinegar
- 3 garlic cloves, minced
- 2 tablespoons cilantro, minced
- 3 teaspoons salt
- 1 (6 ounces) can tomato paste

DIRECTIONS:

1. Combine all ingredients except tomato paste in a large saucepot.

2. Simmer until desired thickness.
3. Stir in tomato paste.
4. Ladle hot salsa into hot jars leaving 1/4 inch head-space.
5. Process 15 minutes in a hot water bath
6. Note: use more hot peppers for a very hot salsa or less for mild.
7. It depends on how hot your peppers are and how hot you like your salsa.
8. I never get close to 2 1/2 cups for our mild salsa.

NUTRITION: Carbohydrates 30.7g; Fat 0.86g; Protein 5.82g; Calories 142

23. Tomatillo Salsa

Preparation Time: 20 minutes

Cooking Time: 10 minutes

Servings: 2 1/2 cups

INGREDIENTS:

- 1 ½ pounds tomatillos (about 12 medium), husked and rinsed
- 1 to 2 medium jalapeños, stemmed (omit for mild salsa, use 1 jalapeño for medium salsa and 2 jalapeños for hot salsa, and note that spiciness will depend on heat of actual peppers used)
- ½ cup chopped white onion (about ½ medium onion)
- ¼ cup packed fresh cilantro leaves (more if you love cilantro)
- 2 tablespoons to ¼ cup lime juice (1 to 2 medium limes, juiced), to taste
- ½ to 1 teaspoon salt, to taste
- Optional variation: 1 to 2 diced avocados, for creamy avocado salsa verde

DIRECTIONS:

1. Preheat the broiler with a rack about 4 inches below the heat source. Place the tomatillos and jalapeño(s) on a rimmed baking sheet and broil until they're blackened in spots, about 5 minutes.
2. Remove the baking sheet from the oven, carefully flip over the tomatillos and pepper(s) with tongs, and broil for 4 to 6 more minutes, until the tomatillos are splotchy-black and blistered.
3. Meanwhile, in a food processor or blender, combine the chopped onion, cilantro, 2 tablespoons lime juice and ½ teaspoon salt. Once the tomatillos are out of the oven, carefully transfer the hot tomatillos, pepper(s) and all of their juices into the food processor or blender.
4. Pulse until the mixture is mostly smooth and no big chunks of tomatillo remain, scraping down the sides as necessary, season to taste with additional lime juice and salt if desired.
5. The salsa will be thinner at first, but will thicken up after a few hours in the refrigerator, due to the naturally occurring pectin in the tomatillos. If you'd like to make creamy avocado salsa verde, let the salsa cool down before blending in 1 to 2 diced avocados (the more avocado, the creamier it gets).

NUTRITION: Carbohydrates 37.58g; Fat 4.57g; Protein 4.32g; Calories 180

Water Bath Canning: Salsas and Relishes

24. Corn & Cherry Tomato Salsa

Preparation Time: 20 minutes

Cooking Time: 10 minutes

Servings: 6 pints

INGREDIENTS:

- 5 pounds cherry tomatoes, roughly chopped
- 2 cups corn kernels (about 2 large ears fresh, but frozen-thawed is fine)
- 1 cup red onion, finely chopped
- 2 teaspoons salt
- ½ cup fresh lime juice (about 3 large or 4 medium limes)
- 2 jalapeño peppers, seeded and minced
- 1 teaspoon chipotle chili powder, optional
- ½ cup chopped fresh cilantro

DIRECTIONS:

1. Prepare the boiling water canner. Heat the jars in simmering water until they're ready for use. Do not boil. Wash the lids in warm soapy water and set them aside with the bands.
2. Bring all the ingredients to a boil in a large stainless-steel or enameled saucepan. Reduce the heat and simmer for 5 to 10 minutes, stirring occasionally.
3. Ladle the hot salsa into a hot jar, leaving ½-inch of headspace. Remove the air bubbles. Wipe the jar rim clean. Center the lid on the jar. Apply the band and adjust to fingertip-tight. Place

the jar in the boiling water canner. Repeat until all the jars are filled.

4. Process the jars for 15 minutes, adjusting for altitude. Turn off the heat; remove the lid, and let the jars stand for 5 minutes. Remove the jars and let them cool.

NUTRITION: Carbohydrates 76.29g; Fat 2.14g; Protein 6.13g; Calories 311

25. Bread and Butter Pickles

Preparation Time: 30 minutes

Cooking Time: 20 minutes

Servings: 3 quarts

INGREDIENTS:

- 15 cups of sliced pickling cucumbers, about 5 pounds; three cups for every pound
- 3 onions sliced thinly
- ¼ cup of salt
- 2 ½ cups of cider vinegar
- 2 ½ cups of sugar
- ¾ teaspoon of turmeric
- ½ teaspoon of celery seed
- 1 tablespoon of mustard seeds
- 6 cups of water

DIRECTIONS:

1. Mix the onions, ice, salt, and cucumbers together in a bowl.
2. Place a plate on top of the bowl with a gallon of water or something heavy on the plate. This serves as a weight. Let it stand for about three hours.
3. After three hours, rinse, and then drain.
4. Mix the sugar, vinegar, celery seed, mustard seed, and turmeric together in a large pot.
5. Add the drained cucumbers.
6. Bring the 6 cups of water almost to a boil in a pot on medium heat.
7. Right at boiling, remove from heat, and seal in the sterilized jars,
8. Place in a hot water bath for 10 minutes.
9. Dry them off, and place on a cookie sheet right side up for around 15 minutes in the oven at 225°F. This is done in order to ensure that there are no air pockets, that everything has been cooked right, and that it is sterilized and sealed properly before being stored. Let cool completely before storing.

NUTRITION: Carbohydrates 106.3g; Fat 5.76g; Protein 9.09g; Calories 492

Water Bath Canning: Salsas and Relishes

Chapter 5: Pressure Canning: Fruits

26. Apple Sauce

Preparation Time: 30 minutes
Cooking Time: 20 minutes
Servings: 4 pints
INGREDIENTS:
- Mix for better flavor, different varieties together.
- 20 big apples
- 4 cups of water
- 2 1/2 cups of sugar

DIRECTIONS:
1. Wash apples; quarter, core; remove any blemishes or any other impurities.
2. If you work in larger lots, drop apples in lemon water, see on acidifying fruit.
3. Upon preparation of all apples, drain if necessary and place in a large cooking pot.
4. Add the four cups of water and cook until apples are soft over medium-high heat.
5. Press a colander to remove peels.
6. Return to the saucepan and add 2 1/2 cups of sugar.
7. Bring the mixture to a boil until the sugar dissolves completely.
8. Pack into boiling hot jars, leaving 1/2 inch of headspace.
9. Wipe the surface with the glass.
10. Screw the lids and rings with.
11. Run for 25 minutes in a boiling bath of water: both pints and quarts.

NUTRITION: Carbohydrates 188.03g; Fat 1.55g; Protein 2.37g; Calories 716

27. Pears

Preparation Time: 30 minutes

Cooking Time: 20 minutes

Servings: 7 half-pints

INGREDIENTS:

- 16 cups (16 medium-size pears) peeled & sliced fresh pears
- 3 tablespoons lemon juice
- 2 cups of water
- 4 cups of sugar

DIRECTIONS:

1. Combine the four ingredients in a large kettle and bring to a boil.
2. Uncover, cook, and stir often for 1 ½ to 2 hours until consistent.
3. Remove from stove and ladle the hot preserves into prepared seven hot sterilized jars with ¼-inch headspace.
4. Take out the air bubbles, make headspace adjustment, and wipe the rims while the center lids on the jars, and screw on the bands.
5. Place the jars in the boiling water in the canner and boil for ten minutes. Remove the hot jars; let cool on top of a towel.
6. Enjoy!

NUTRITION: Carbohydrates 21g; Fat 0g; Protein 0g

28. Strawberries

Preparation Time: 30 minutes

Cooking Time: 20 minutes

Servings: 7 half-pints

INGREDIENTS:

- 1 cup of sugar
- About 2 pounds of strawberries
- 1/2 cup of strawberry juice

DIRECTIONS:

1. Wash the strawberries.
2. Sort through berries, pick bruised, damaged, and too soft ones and put them aside.
3. Remove the roots, bruises, and damage from beers of poor quality.
4. Crush those berries and heat them up to get the juice.
5. Use a sieve to drain the juice from the berries.
6. Back to the pan.
7. Add sugar to the milk and simmer for 3 minutes.
8. Set aside to freshen up.
9. To canned stem berries; to put them in a large, non-reactive bowl or pot.
10. Set aside to about room temperature until juice has cooled.
11. Pour juice over berries, cover, and set aside for 3-5 hours, if the juice has cooled sufficiently.
12. Pack in jars to within 1/2 inch of the top after this point.

Pressure Canning: Fruits

13. Make sure that juice is split evenly between the jars.
14. Screw and rings on the lid.
15. Add method in boiling bathwater: both 15 minutes of pints and quarts.

NUTRITION: Carbohydrates 26.52g; Fat 0.42g; Protein 0.92g; Calories 107

Pressure Canning: Fruits

Chapter 6: Pressure Canning: Vegetables

29. Glazed Carrots

Preparation Time: 30 minutes

Cooking/pressurizing Time: 50 minutes

Servings: 6 pint jars (12 cups)

INGREDIENTS:

- 6-7 pounds of carrots
- 2 cups of brown sugar
- 2 cups of water
- 1 cup of orange juice
- 1 tablespoon kosher salt

DIRECTIONS:

1. Wash, peel, and slice carrots. Slices should be thick 1-2-inch. Mix brown sugar with water and orange juice as well as the carrots in a large saucepot. Bring to a boil. Reduce heat to

medium, and cook until the sugar has dissolved and carrots are almost tender about 10-15 minutes.
2. Pack the carrots into the jars, and pour the syrup over the carrots.
3. Process pints and quarts at 10 pounds each for 30 minutes for the weighted gauge of the pressure canner or 11 pounds if the pressure canner has a dial gauge.
4. Remove jars, and let them cool completely at room temperature before storing. This can take about a day.

NUTRITION: Carbohydrates 39.22g; Fat 0.47g; Protein 2.01g; Calories 161

30. Green Beans

Preparation Time: 30 minutes

Cooking Time: 20 minutes

Servings: 1 quart

INGREDIENTS:

- 2 lb. of green beans per quart
- Water
- Salt, optional
- Ball® Glass preserving jars with lids and bands

*****You must process at least 2-quart jars or 4-pint jars in the pressure canner at one time to ensure safe processing.**

DIRECTIONS:

1. Prepare pressure canner. Heat jars in simmering water until ready for use. Do not boil. Wash lids in warm soapy water and set bands aside.

2. Wash and rinse beans thoroughly. Remove string, trim ends and break or cut freshly gathered beans into 2-inch pieces.

Place prepared beans in a large saucepan and cover with boiling water. Boil for 5 minutes.

3. Pack hot beans into hot jars leaving 1-inch headspace. Add 1 tsp. salt to each quart jar, 1/2 tsp. to each pint jar, if desired.
4. Ladle boiling water over beans leaving 1-inch headspace. Remove air bubbles. Wipe rim. Center hot lid on jar. Apply band and adjust until fit is fingertip tight.
5. Process filled jars in a pressure canner at 10 pounds pressure 20 minutes for pints and 25 minutes for quarts, adjusting for altitude. Remove jars and cool. Check lids for seal after 24 hours. The lid should not flex up and down when the center is pressed.

TIP: The processing time given applies only to young, tender pods. Beans that have almost reached the "shell-out" stage require a longer time for processing. Increase processing time 15 minutes for pints and 20 minutes for quarts.

NUTRITION: Carbohydrates 33.16g; Fat 0.91g; Protein 6.35g; Calories 168

Pressure Canning: Vegetables

31. Tomatoes

Preparation Time: 30 minutes

Cooking Time: 20 minutes

Servings: 7 quarts

INGREDIENTS:

- 21 pounds whole tomatoes, skinned
- 4 tablespoons of salt
- ¾ cup lemon juice, optional
- Boiling water

DIRECTIONS:

1. Place the tomatoes and the salt in a saucepan and cover with the water. Bring to a boil and cook for 5 minutes.
2. Pack sterilized jars with the tomatoes and the hot liquid; leaving a ½ inch headspace, remove any air bubbles, clean the rim and adjust lids.
3. If omitting the lemon juice, process the jars for 45 minutes in a pressure canner at 10 pounds of pressure for a pressure canner with a weighted gauge or 11 pounds if the pressure canner has a dial gauge.
4. If using lemon juice, process the jars for 10 minutes in a boiling water bath.

NUTRITION: Carbohydrates 42.36g; Fat 3.6g; Protein 13.43g; Calories 210

32. Stewed Tomatoes

Preparation Time: 20 minutes

Cooking/pressurizing Time: 40 minutes

Servings: 4-pint jars or 2-quart jars

INGREDIENTS:

- 4 quarts red tomatoes, around 16-18 medium-size tomatoes
- 1 yellow onion, diced
- ½ green pepper, diced
- 4 teaspoons of celery salt
- 4 teaspoons of sugar
- 1 teaspoon of salt

DIRECTIONS:

1. Wash tomatoes. Blanch the tomatoes for 1-2 minutes in boiling water. Drain the water, and let cool until you can manipulate

the tomatoes with your fingers. Remove the skin, and chop the tomatoes.
2. Combine all ingredients into the saucepan, and bring to a boil. Reduce the heat to low. Cover, and let simmer gently for 12-15 minutes, stirring often, until it starts to get a bit thicker.
3. Pack the mixture equally into jars.
4. Process 15 minutes for pints at 11 pounds or 20 minutes for quarts at 10 pounds for the weighted gauge of the pressure canner or 11 pounds if the pressure canner has a dial gauge.
5. Remove the jars, and let cool until at room temperature before storing. This can take up to a day.

NUTRITION: Carbohydrates 9.59g; Fat 2.61g; Protein 1.42g; Calories 63

33. Herbed Peas

Preparation Time: 30 minutes
Cooking Time: 20 minutes
Servings: 4 pints

INGREDIENTS:

- 3 lbs. of peas
- Chervil
- Thyme
- Water

DIRECTIONS:

1. You will use the pressure canner with this one. Wash and dry peas and shell and wash again.
2. Boil the peas, pack hot peas in jars, and add seasoning and can using a pressure cooker.

NUTRITION: Carbohydrates 25.81g; Fat 0.69g; Protein 9.57g; Calories 143

34. Herbed Tomatoes

Preparation Time: 30 minutes

Cooking Time: 20 minutes

Servings: 4 pints

INGREDIENTS:

1. 8 lbs. tomatoes, peeled
2. Water
3. Spiced blend (house seasoning)

DIRECTIONS:

1. Combine tomatoes and water in a saucepan and let boil.
2. Add spices and add to canning tomatoes and use pressure cooking method.

NUTRITION: Carbohydrates 46.46g; Fat 4.2g; Protein 10.28g; Calories 238

35. Asparagus

Preparation Time: 30 minutes
Cooking Time: 20 minutes
Servings: 9 pints

INGREDIENTS:

- 16 pounds asparagus spears
- 10 tablespoons salt
- Boiling water

DIRECTIONS:

1. In a large pot, cover the asparagus with the boiling water and add the salt. Boil for 3 minutes. Fill sterilized jars loosely with the asparagus and liquid, leaving 1-inch headspace.
2. Adjust the jar lids and process the jars for 30 minutes in a pressure canner at 10 pounds of pressure for a pressure canner with a weighted gauge or 11 pounds if the pressure canner has a dial gauge.

NUTRITION: Carbohydrates 31.29g; Fat 0.97g; Protein 17.74g; Calories 161

36. Marinated Mushrooms

Preparation Time: 30 minutes

Cooking Time: 20 minutes

Servings: 9 pints

INGREDIENTS:

- Pimiento, diced (1/4 cup)
- Lemon juice, bottled (1/2 cup)
- Basil leaves, dried (1 tablespoon)
- White vinegar, 5% (2 ½ cups)
- Onions, chopped finely (1/2 cup)
- Mushrooms, small, whole (7 pounds)
- Oil, olive/salad (2 cups)
- Oregano leaves (1 tablespoon)
- Pickling/canning salt (1 tablespoon)
- Black peppercorns (25 pieces)

DIRECTIONS:

1. Make sure your mushrooms are very fresh, still unopened, and have caps with a diameter of less than 1 ¼ inches.
2. Wash the mushrooms before cutting the stems, but leave a quarter of an inch still attached to their caps. Put in a saucepan and cover with water and lemon juice. Heat until boiling, and then simmer for five minutes before draining.

3. Add the vinegar, salt, basil, oregano, and olive oil to a saucepan. Stir to combine as you also add the pimiento and onions. Heat the mixture until boiling.
4. Meanwhile, fill each of your clean and hot Mason jars (half-pint) with garlic clove (1/4 portion) and peppercorns (2 to 3 pieces)/ Add the cooked mushrooms as well as the hot liquid mixture, making sure to leave half an inch of headspace.
5. Take out any air bubbles before adjusting the lids. Place in the pressure canner and process for twenty minutes.

TIPS: You can process your foods without salt. Use canning salt if you want to add salt to your pressure canned foods. You can add one-half teaspoon of canning salt to each pint jar (if using quart jars, add one teaspoon).

NUTRITION: Carbohydrates 2.97g; Fat 48.25g; Protein 0.49g; Calories 451

Pressure Canning: Vegetables

Chapter 7: Pressure Canning: Meat, Poultry, and Seafood

37. Canned Chicken

Preparation Time: 30 minutes

Cooking/pressurizing Time: 2 hours

Servings: 8-pint jars

INGREDIENTS:

- 18 medium boneless and skinless chicken breasts
- 1 ½ tablespoon of salt
- 4 ½ cups of water
- Butter or Olive Oil for frying in a skillet

DIRECTIONS:

1. Cook each side of the chicken in a skillet with some butter or olive oil, about 8-10 minutes. Remove from heat when the chicken is white and cooked all the way through. If you poke it with a fork, the juices run clear.
2. In each pint jar place a ½ teaspoon of salt and 2 chicken breasts.
3. Fill the jar with water, process for 70 minutes at 10 pounds of pressure for the weighted gauge of the pressure canner or 11 pounds if the pressure canner has a dial gauge.
4. Remove jars, and let cool until it is room temperature, which may take about a day.

NUTRITION: Carbohydrates 0g; Fat 55.09g; Protein 5.06g; Calories 509

38. Mexican Turkey Soup

Preparation Time: 20 minutes

Cooking/pressurizing Time: 1 hour and 30 minutes

Servings: 8-quart jars or 16-pint jars

INGREDIENTS:

- 6 cups of cooked turkey, chopped
- 2 cups of chopped onions
- 8 ounces can of Mexican green chilies, chopped and drained
- ¼ cup of taco seasoning mix, packed
- 28 ounces of crushed tomatoes with the juices
- 16 cups of turkey or chicken broth
- 3 cups of corn
- 1 ½ tablespoon of extra virgin olive oil

DIRECTIONS:

1. In a large stockpot, warm olive oil on medium-high heat. Sauté the onions until tender and fragrant, about 2 minutes on medium-high heat. Reduce heat to medium-low.
2. Add taco seasoning and the chilies. Cook and stir for another 3 minutes, add in the tomatoes and the broth. Bring to a boil, and then add the corn and the turkey.
3. Reduce heat to low, and let simmer for 10 minutes.
4. Ladle equally into the jars.
5. Process pints at 10 pounds for 75 minutes and quarts at 10 pounds for 90 minutes for the weighted gauge of the pressure canner or 11 pounds if the pressure canner has a dial gauge.
6. Remove jars, and let cool until it is at room temperature. This may take about a day.

NUTRITION: Carbohydrates 30.08g; Fat 76.84g; Protein 63.66g; Calories 1079

39. Fish

Preparation Time: 20 minutes

Cooking/pressurizing Time: 1 hour and 30 minutes

Servings: 5 pints

INGREDIENTS:

- 5 pounds tuna or salmon
- 5-pint sized mason jars with lids and rings
- Canning salt
- Lemon juice
- 1 jalapeño pepper

DIRECTIONS:

1. Place 1 slice of jalapeño pepper into each jar.
2. Fill jars with meat to ½ inch from the top.
3. Add ¼ tsp. canning salt and 1 tsp. lemon juice per pint.
4. Use a knife to jiggle meat and remove any air pockets.
5. Wipe rim of jar clean.
6. Heat lids in hot water for 3 minutes; place lids on jars and tighten rings slightly.
7. Place jars in the canner and fill with water to the jar rings.
8. Close and lock pressure canner and bring to a boil over high heat, then add cooking weight to the top.
9. After 20 minutes, turn heat to medium and cook for 75 minutes.

10. Turn off heat and leave canner alone until it has cooled completely to room temperature.
11. After canner has cooled, remove jars from the canner and check for sealing.
12. If jars have sealed, store for up to 2 years; if not, use meat right away.

NUTRITION: Carbohydrates 1.51g; Fat 32.56g; Protein 93.79g; Calories 700

40. Chicken Cacciatore

Preparation time: 20 minutes

Cooking time: 20 minutes

Servings: 8-10 pints

INGREDIENTS:

- 3 tablespoons olive oil
- 8 large breasts boneless, skinless chicken breasts, cut into 2-inch cubes (8 cups)
- 12 boneless, skinless chicken thighs, cut into 2-inch pieces (6 cups)
- 1 tablespoon dried oregano
- 1 tablespoon dried basil
- 1 teaspoon dried thyme
- 1 teaspoon dried rosemary, crushed
- 1 teaspoon coarse sea salt
- ½ teaspoon ground black pepper
- 1 cup red wine
- 4 cups diced tomatoes, with their juice
- 4 cups tomato juice
- 2 cups sliced white mushrooms
- 3 cups coarsely chopped sweet onion
- 1 large red bell pepper, chopped (1½ cups)
- 1 celery stalk, chopped (½ cup)
- 6 garlic cloves, minced
- ¾ cup tomato paste (6 ounces)
- 1 tablespoon granulated sugar

DIRECTIONS:

1. In a thick-bottomed stockpot, combine the oil and the chicken breasts and thighs. Mix well to coat the chicken. Cook the chicken on medium-high heat for 3 minutes, stirring often. Add

the oregano, basil, thyme, rosemary, salt, and pepper. Mix well and cook for an additional 3 minutes. Add the red wine, cover the stockpot, and let cook for 5 more minutes undisturbed.

2. Add the tomatoes, Tomato Juice, mushrooms, onion, bell pepper, celery, and garlic. Mix well and bring to a boil. Boil for 5 minutes. Add the tomato paste and sugar, mixing well to distribute paste. Boil for an additional 5 minutes. Remove from the heat.

3. Using a slotted spoon, fill each hot jar three-quarters full with the chicken and vegetables. Ladle the hot tomato sauce over the mixture, leaving 1 inch of headspace. Remove any air bubbles and add additional sauce if necessary to maintain the 1 inch of headspace.

4. Wipe the rim of each jar with a warm washcloth dipped in distilled white vinegar. Place a lid and ring on each jar and hand tighten.

5. Place jars in the pressure canner, lock the pressure canner lid and bring to a boil on high heat. Let the canner vent for 10 minutes. Close the vent and continue heating to achieve 11 PSI for a dial gauge and 10 PSI for a weighted gauge. Process quart jars for 1 hour 30 minutes and pint jars for 1 hour 15 minutes.

Serving Tip: This dish is traditionally served over pasta noodles, flat or spaghetti, and topped with fresh chopped parsley and shaved Parmesan cheese. For a fun kick, use V8® juice, regular or spicy, instead of Tomato Juice.

NUTRITION: Carbohydrates 42.14g; Fat 43.8g; Protein 37.12g; Calories 701

Pressure Canning: Meat, Poultry, and Seafood

Chapter 8: Pressure Canning: Soups, Stews

41. Cabbage Soup

Preparation time: 30 minutes
Cooking time: 1 hour and 15 minutes
Servings: 9 pints

INGREDIENTS:

- 2 kg of minced meat
- 1 large onion, diced
- 2 garlic cloves, minced
- 6 cups of cabbage, grated
- 1 cup diced celery
- 1 cup diced green pepper
- 2 cans of light beans (16 ounces)
- 8 glasses of canned tomatoes with juice (2 liters if you can make your own like me)
- 10 cubes of veal broth
- 8 cups of water
- 2 tablespoons of garlic powder
- 20 rounds of fresh peppercorn (I use it)
- 2 teaspoons of sea salt
- 1 tablespoon of dried parsley
- 2 tablespoons of dried basil
- 1 tablespoon of thyme
- 1 teaspoon dried celery

DIRECTIONS:

Sterilizing

- Sterilize to prepare glass jars, lids, and rings. Chop and cut all the vegetables and set aside. Collect all the dry ingredients and set them aside

Cooking:

1. **Minced meat:** brown minced meat in a pan so far pink. Separate 3 tablespoons of onion and garlic fat. If desired, drain and wash the meat to remove excess oil.
2. **Prepare the beef:** heat 8 cups of water in a large bowl or use 2-liter jars filled with water in each jar - 5 cubes of beef broth.
3. Microwave for 5 minutes to dissolve the cubes. Remove it carefully, it will be very hot, stir quickly to make sure the cubes are thawed.
4. **Sautéed onion and garlic:** pour 3 tablespoons of fat in a large saucepan and wrap the chopped onions and fry the garlic until tender.
5. **Mix with other ingredients:** add cooked minced meat, cabbage, celery, green pepper, beans, fruit juice, tomato, and broth - mix well.
6. **Mix all the dry ingredients:** garlic powder, pepper, sea salt, parsley, basil, thyme, and celery. Boil, and cook for 20 minutes. Actually, your soup is ready to eat at this point.

Filling jars:

- **Note:** protect the counter by using a cloth or towel to adjust the jars since you will fill the hot jars. Make use of a spoon strainer to fill the jars with half-filled solids, then fill the rest of the jar with water up to 1 inch in the cavity. Using a clean, damp cloth, remove any particles or water from the edge of the glass jar, insert the lid and ring and squeeze with your finger. When filling each can, place it in the pressure container. Make sure to place the shelf under the can.

Processing:

7. Place the lid on the box and lock it. Set the temperature to high. Vent the steam for it

NUTRITION: Carbohydrates 101.88g; Fat 7.44g; Protein 88.47g; Calories 773

42. Beef Stew

Preparation time: 30 minutes
Cooking time: 15 minutes
Servings: 7 quarts or 14 pints

INGREDIENTS:

- 2 tablespoons of extra-virgin olive oil, divided
- 5 pounds of stew beef, cut into bite-size pieces
- 10 cups of potatoes, peeled and cubed
- 8 cups of medium carrots, peeled and chopped
- 3 cups of chopped onions
- 2 cups of chopped celery
- 6 medium Roma tomatoes, diced (3 cups)
- 4½ teaspoons of coarse sea salt (optional)
- 1 tablespoon of dried parsley
- 1 tablespoon of dried oregano
- ½ tablespoon of celery seeds
- 1 teaspoon of ground coriander
- 1 teaspoon of dried thyme
- 1 teaspoon of dried basil
- ½ teaspoon of ground black pepper
- 8 cups of Beef Broth
- 5 cups of water

DIRECTIONS:

1. In a thick-bottomed stockpot, heat 1 tablespoon oil and brown the beef in batches until all the beef is lightly browned, about 3 to 5 minutes per batch. Add 1 additional tablespoon of oil while browning each batch. Remove each batch from the stockpot and place it in a bowl. Be sure not to fully cook the beef.

2. Return the browned beef to the stockpot and add the potatoes, carrots, onions, celery, tomatoes, salt (if using), parsley, oregano, celery seeds, coriander, thyme, basil, and pepper and mix well. Add the Beef Broth and water and mix well. Bring to a boil over medium-high heat, stirring frequently. Let it boil for 5 minutes then remove from the heat.

3. Ladle the hot stew into hot jars, leaving 1 inch of headspace. Remove any air bubbles and add additional stew if necessary, to maintain the 1 inch of headspace.

4. Wipe the rim of each jar with a warm washcloth dipped in distilled white vinegar. Place a lid and ring on each jar and hand tighten.

5. Place jars in the pressure canner, lock the pressure canner lid and bring to a boil on high heat. Let the canner vent for 10 minutes. Close the vent and continue heating to achieve 11 PSI for a dial gauge and 10 PSI for a weighted gauge. Process quart jars for 1 hour 30 minutes and pint jars for 1 hour 15 minutes.

INGREDIENT TIP: Using a pressure canner makes even the toughest cuts of meat tender and flavorful. Beef sold for stew typically comes from the chuck or round roasts, cut into 1½-inch pieces. Bottom and eye cuts, also known as round, are typically leaner than a chuck roast, which are cuts from the shoulder, leg, and butt. When cutting into bite-size pieces, cut to a size you would feel comfortable seeing on the end of your fork or spoon.

NUTRITION: Carbohydrates 55.14g; Fat 16.38g; Protein 81.16g; Calories 680

43. Potato and Leek Soup

Preparation time: 30 minutes

Cooking time: 15 minutes

Servings: 7 quarts or 14 pints

INGREDIENTS:

- 6 potatoes, peeled and cubed
- 4 cups stock, chicken or beef
- 5 pounds leeks, washed and cut into ¼-inch slices

DIRECTIONS:

1. Layer leaks at the bottom of each jar. Place a layer of potatoes on top of the leeks, followed by another layer of the sliced leeks.
2. Boil the chicken or beef stock before pouring into the jars. Make sure to leave about an inch of space at the top of each jar.
3. Attach the lids to the jars and process in a pressure canner using 11 pounds for 60 minutes.

NUTRITION: Carbohydrates 101.1g; Fat 2.34g; Protein 14.26g; Calories 462

44. Veggie Soup

Preparation time: 60 minutes

Cooking time: 15 minutes

Servings: 9-pint jars

INGREDIENTS:

- 6 cups tomatoes (cored, peeled, chopped)
- 2 cups of tomatillos (chopped)
- 1 cup of onion (chopped)
- 1 cup of carrots (chopped)
- 1 cup of green bell pepper (chopped)
- 1 cup of red bell pepper (chopped)
- 6 cups of corn kernels
- ½ cup hot pepper (seeded, chopped)
- 1 teaspoon cayenne pepper
- 5 cups tomato juice
- 1 tablespoon hot sauce
- 2 teaspoon chili powder
- 2 teaspoon cumin (ground)
- 1 teaspoon salt
- 2 cups of water
- 1 teaspoon black pepper

DIRECTIONS:

1. Sterilize the jars
2. Combine all the ingredients in a pot and bring to boil.
3. Simmer uncovered for 15 minutes on low flame.
4. Distribute the solids and liquid among the jars, leaving one inch of headspace.
5. Get rid of any air bubbles and clean the rims.

6. Cover the jars with the lid and apply the bands making sure that it is tightened.
7. Process the jars for 60 minutes at 10 pounds pressure in a pressure canner.
8. Remove; allow cooling, and then labeling the jars.

NUTRITION: Calories: 185; Fat: 1.9g; Carbohydrates: 42.8g; Proteins: 6.9g

45. Fennel & Carrot Soup

Preparation time: 35 minutes

Cooking time: 30 minutes

Servings: 9-pint jars

INGREDIENTS:

- 1 lb. of fennel bulbs (trimmed)
- 1 tablespoon of olive oil
- 4 ½ lbs. of carrots (peeled, sliced)
- 12 cups of vegetable stock
- 2 teaspoon of onion powder
- 2 tablespoons of salt
- 1 teaspoon of dried ginger (ground)
- 1 teaspoon of dried thyme
- ½ teaspoon of cumin (ground)
- 3 tablespoons of lemon juice
- 1 teaspoon of black pepper (ground)
- 1 teaspoon of dried coriander (ground)

DIRECTIONS:

1. Sterilize the jars
2. Heat oil in a pot and sauté the fennel in it till translucent.
3. Mix in the carrots and 4 cups vegetable broth and simmer for 30 minutes.
4. Leave to cool, and then puree the mixture.
5. Return to the pot and mix in the remainder of the ingredients.
6. Bring to boil and simmer for 20-30 minutes.

7. Ladle the mix immediately into the sterilized jars, leaving one inch of headspace.
8. Get rid of any air bubbles and clean the rims.
9. Cover the jars with the lid and apply the bands making sure that it is tightened.
10. Process the jars for 35 minutes at 10 pounds pressure in a pressure canner.
11. Remove; allow cooling, and then labeling the jars.

NUTRITION: Calories 48; Fat 0.7g; Carbohydrates 10.1g; Proteins 2.8g

46. Tomato Soup

Preparation time: 30 minutes

Cooking time: 20 minutes

Servings: 18-pint jars

INGREDIENTS:

- 15 lbs. of tomatoes (chopped roughly)
- 2 tablespoons of olive oil
- 3 cups of celery (chopped)
- 3 cups of onions (chopped)
- 1 tablespoon of salt
- 1 tablespoon of pepper
- 64 oz. of vegetable stock
- ¼ cup of garlic (chopped)
- 32 oz. of water
- 2 cups of carrots (chopped)

DIRECTIONS:

1. Sterilize the jars
2. Heat olive oil in a pot and sauté the onions, celery, and carrots in it.
3. Mix in the tomatoes, salt, pepper, stock, and water and leave to simmer for 2 hours.
4. Pour the soup using an immersion blender.
5. Ladle the mix immediately into the sterilized jars, leaving one inch of headspace.
6. Get rid of any air bubbles and clean the rims.

7. Cover the jars with the lid and apply the bands making sure that it is tightened.
8. Submerge the jars within a prepared boiling water canner and leave to process for 20 minutes.
9. Remove; allow cooling, and then labeling the jars.

NUTRITION: Calories: 63.4; Fat: 1.7g; Carbohydrates: 10g; Proteins: 1.8g

47. Chicken Soup

Preparation time: 30 minutes
Cooking time: 20 minutes
Servings: 8-pint jars

INGREDIENTS:

- 3 cups of chicken (diced)
- 6 cups of chicken broth
- 10 cups of water
- 1 cup of onion (diced)
- Salt and pepper to taste
- 1 ½ cups of celery (diced)
- 1 ½ cups of carrots (sliced)
- 3 chicken bouillon cubes

DIRECTIONS:

1. Sterilize the jars
2. Combine all the ingredients in a pot except the salt, pepper, and bouillon cubes and bring to boil.
3. Reduce the flame and simmer for 30 minutes.
4. Stir in the remaining ingredients and stir cook until the bouillon cubes dissolve.
5. Turn off the flame and skim-off any visible foam.
6. Ladle the mix immediately into the sterilized jars, leaving one inch of headspace.
7. Get rid of any air bubbles and clean the rims.
8. Cover the jars with the lid and apply the bands making sure that it is tightened.
9. Process the jars for 1 hour 15 minutes at 10 pounds pressure in a pressure canner.
10. Remove; allow cooling, and then labeling the jars.

NUTRITION: Calories: 75.4; Fat: 0.3g; Carbohydrates: 5.4g; Proteins: 12.2g

Pressure Canning: Soups, Stews

Chapter 9: Fermenting

The Process of Fermentation

Food Fermentation isn't rocket science. You don't need to have a food fermentation factory to do so, and you also don't need lots of cash just to be able to ferment food. In fact, you can do it in the comforts of your own home and that's one of the best things about it.

So, how exactly can you ferment food? What are the basic ways of doing so? Here's what you need to know:

1. **Choose your equipment.** Of course, before you start the process of food fermentation, you should first have the right equipment with you. Mason Jars are definitely needed, as well as good kinds of knives that you can use to prepare the vegetables. Most of the equipment that you may need are as follows:

   - **Fermenting Vessel.** This is where you'll place those vegetables or condiments. It's a general rule that cylindrical-shaped containers are better than other shapes because it's easier to ferment in them. Examples of Fermenting Vessels include:
     1. Ceramic Crocks
     2. Ceramic Fermenting Crocks
     3. Canning Jars
     4. Slow Cooker Inserts
     5. Mason/Glass Jars
     6. Ceramic or Glass Bowls

7. Glass Jars with Airlock Systems

- **Weights and Covers.** You also need equipment that will cover the food for you and this always depends on what food you'll be fermenting. For example, Vegetables in brine are required to have weight and cover systems, whereas vegetables, fruits, and condiments without brine can be prepared simply by just placing a lid on the container and waiting for them to be fermented. Examples of Weights and Covers include:
    1. Ceramic Fermentation Weights
    2. Heavy Glass
    3. Ceramic Coasters
    4. Small jars
    5. Small plates

2. **Method of Preparation.** Next, you should also decide on which method of preparation you'll use to ferment the food that you have on hand. This differs based on the ingredients that you have with you and you have to know which method is best suited for what you have with you. Some of these methods are:

- **Chopping.** When you chop vegetables or fruits, you have to be sure that they'll be in bite-sized pieces, so you can easily eat them right away. Examples of vegetables that you can chop include summer squash, cucumber, peppers, green beans, asparagus, eggplant, and carrots.

- **Grating.** Grated fruits or vegetables are very smooth and come only in extremely small but somewhat lengthy pieces. You can either do this by hand or with the help of a food processor. Usually, these are done for those that you want to make as relish or sides. Examples include cabbage, zucchini, cucumber, beets, turnips, radish, and carrot.

- **Slicing.** Slicing fruits or vegetables increases surface area and is best done for Sauerkraut and those fruits or vegetables that you'll soak in the brine. They also make culturing time faster. Examples include celery, peppers, zucchini, cucumbers, and cabbage.

3. **Culturing**. Culturing, or the use of whey, salt, and other kinds of starters is the act of choosing which starter culture is best for whatever it is that you want to make. Oftentimes, they determine the length of time for those foods to be fermented and you need starter cultures to inhibit the growth of undesirable bacteria or organisms that may stall the fermentation process. Examples of starter cultures include:

- **Salt**. Salt has always been the classic culture for fermenting food and it has been used even before refrigeration was around. Salt pulls undesired bacteria away and takes moisture out of the food that you're preparing so that it will last for a long time. It also suppresses the growth of organisms that you don't actually need. 1 to 3 Tablespoons of salt for every quart of water is the recommended ratio.

- **Fermented Juice**. Basically, this is the juice or the liquid taken from food that you have fermented earlier. You just have to add around ¼ cup of it to the new mixture, together with salt brine to make fermentation easier.

- **Whey**. Whey is kind of tricky because it may work for others but may not work for the rest. If you're going to use whey, make sure that it tastes fresh and that it has been strained properly. Whey's great though, in the sense that it keeps the natural crunchiness of vegetables intact.

4. **Water Source**. It's a given fact that you need brine to ferment most types of food, but where exactly should the water you'll use come from? Here are some water sources that you can choose from:

- **Tap Water**. Basically, tap water is water that comes out of the faucet. It can either be mineral-rich or on the other hand, it could also be free of any minerals. You may have to run this through a water softener first just to make sure that it's safe.

- **Spring Water**. Spring water usually comes in bottles but is originally from the ground—which makes it rich in minerals and makes it healthy!

- **Distilled Water**. Distilled Water contains no minerals and has been thoroughly purified. You can usually buy this from your water supply store or from the supermarket.

- **Bottled Water**. This can either be mineral water, spring or distilled. Just check the label to be sure what of it is.

5. **Keeping them safe**. When you're trying to ferment vegetables, you want to be sure that they stay in place so that the

fermentation process won't be interrupted. Some of the things that you can use to keep them safe are:

- **A small dish**. Put a small dish on top of the vegetables and make sure that brine covers it as well. Then, place another small heavy item on top of the dish to keep it even safer.
- **Cabbage or Kale leaf**. Actually, any strong piece of a vegetable leaf will do. Just tuck it on top of the vegetables and it will already be able to keep the vegetables in place. Carrot or Zucchini strips can work, too.
- **Ceramic Fermentation Weights.** These are basically made for the process of fermentation so you can never go wrong with them.
- **Glass Stones**. You know, those stones that you usually use to decorate the aquarium or your floral arrangements with—they are these stones. Make sure though that they're really clean before you put them on top of the vegetables. Choose ones that are over 2 inches in diameter, so you won't have a hard time.
- **Fermenting in a bowl before transferring to jars**. If you can't make use of the methods given above, it's also okay to ferment the vegetables in a bowl first then just use a large plate to press them down. Once they're done or are fully submerged, move them to the storage jars together with their brine.

6. **Ready for the move**. Finally, once you have done all the techniques above, it's time for the vegetables to be transferred into cold storage. However, this may be tricky because not

everyone knows if the food's actually ready to be moved or not. Well, here are some signs that will allow you to know if you can already transfer the vegetables to cold storage:

- **The Smell.** It's true that you'll know whether a food is good or not through its aroma. Well, you'll also know whether a food is already close to being fermented or not by means of smelling it and by the aroma that it emits. If your fermented food is ready, it should have this vinegary-sour smell. At first, the smell may be too strong, then you'll notice that it will subside after a couple of seconds or so. However, when you think that it smells rotten, chances are it probably is, so just throw it away and start all over again.

- **Bubbles.** Seeing bubbles in your fermented foods are also normal because it means that lactic acid has been formed and that the vegetables are being cultured. Take note though, that the amount and size of bubbles will differ for each food product so know that even though zucchini has more bubbles than tomatoes, there's no problem with it.

- **Flavor.** And of course, the flavor is very important, too. Now, when you've smelled that sour smell and when you've seen the bubbles, you should get on to taste what you have made. Once you notice that it's already flavorful or tangy, especially for pickles, you can then transfer them to cold storage. Congratulations!

7. **And, beware of molds.** As you're going to ferment these fruits and vegetables, you should also be aware that molds may form,

and once they do, you have to discard what you have made and just begin again. Molds usually appear because of a variety of things and some of them are:

- **The Quality of Fruits and Vegetables**. Of course, when you see that the fruits and vegetables you have on hand are about to decay, why in the world would you still use them? That's just like you're inviting molds to invade them!

- **The amount of salt**. 1 to 3 Tablespoons of salt per quart of water is good, but anything more (or less) than that may just bring on bad bacteria and molds, so always be aware of how much salt you're putting in.

- **Vegetable Submersion**. You can prevent molds from infesting your vegetables if you actually submerge them well in water and if you won't allow oxygen to come in contact with them while they're in the fermenting vessel.

- **The Temperature**. It's best to ferment food in a cool place because this will prevent molds from being around, and it'll also make the whole process faster and easier. 65 to 70F is recommended.

Fermenting

Chapter 10: Freezing

Freezing and refrigeration are the most common types of preservation in homes around the world today. Where refrigeration slows bacterial action, freezing comes close to totally stopping microbes' development. This happens because the water in frozen food turns to ice, in which bacteria cannot continue to grow. Enzyme activity, on the other hand, isn't completely deterred by freezing, which is why many vegetables are blanched before being packaged. Once an item is defrosted completely, however, any microbes still within will begin to grow again.

What Can Be Frozen?

Except for eggs in the shell, nearly all foods can be frozen raw, after blanching and/or cooking. So the real question here is what foods don't take well to freezing. The following list includes the foods you generally cannot freeze:

- Cream sauces separate even when warmed completely after being frozen.
- Mayonnaise, cream cheese, and cottage cheese don't hold up well, often losing textural quality.
- Milk seems to be a 50-50 proposition. While it can be frozen quite safely, it sometimes separates after being frozen. If remixed, this milk is an option for cooking and baking.
- Precooked meat can be frozen, but it doesn't have as much moisture as raw and will often dry out further if left frozen for more than four weeks.

Freezing

- Cured meats don't last long in the freezer and should be used in less than four weeks.

If you're ever in doubt about how to best prepare an item for freezing (or even if you should), the National Center for Home Preserving **(www.uga.edu/nchfp)** is a great online resource. It offers tips on how to freeze various items ranging from pie and prepared food to oysters and artichokes.

Frosty Facts

In freezing, zero is your magic number. At 0°F, microbes become dormant. The food won't spoil, and any germs therein will not breed until you defrost the food. Bear in mind, though, that the longer the food remains frozen the more it tends to lose certain qualities such as vivid flavor and texture. Always try to freeze things when they're at their peak and remember that cooking your defrosted food as soon as it's thawed will also stop microbial growth.

The first step in freezing is keeping those items cold until you're ready to prepare them. This is very important with meat, but it also makes a difference in how fruits and vegetables come out of the freezer.

1. Equipment

Once you're ready to begin, assemble all the items you need. For example, if you're freezing fruit, you'll want a clean cutting board, a sharp knife, and your choice of storage containers. If you're doing any preparation on the fruit before freezing it, you'll also need cooking pans. Stainless steel is highly recommended; galvanized pans may give off zinc when the fruit is left in them because of the fruit's acid content. Additionally, there's nothing like stainless steel for easy cleanup.

If it's in your budget, a vacuum sealer is another great piece of equipment to consider. Vacuum sealers come in a variety of sizes with a similar variety of bags that are perfect for preservers who like freezing and drying methods. They're fairly cost-effective when compared to freezer bags or plastic containers, and they eliminate the excess air that contributes to ice crystals.

A third item that you shouldn't be without is a freezer-proof label system. If you double-wrap your frozen items, put a label on each layer. If one gets knocked off, the other remains.

2. Help and Hints

Freezing, like any other method of preservation, requires some observation and annotation to achieve success. As you're working with recipes, remember that practice really does make perfect. For example, you may follow a recipe for frozen butter pickles exactly, but you find you'd like the cucumbers sliced more thinly for greater flavor. Make a note of that and change it next time.

As you note changes you'd like to make, also consider if that means getting different types of equipment for your kitchen. In the case of the cucumbers and other thinly sliced vegetables, a mandolin might be the perfect fix. Put it on a wish list. Being prepared saves a lot of last-minute headaches, and having the right tools is always a great boon.

3. Vegetables

Vegetables should be chosen for crispness and freshness. Home gardeners should pick their items a few hours before packing them for the ultimate in organic goodness. The next step for vegetables is blanching, which will improve the lifespan of your frozen goods.

If there's no specific blanching time provided in your preserving recipe, here's a brief overview to get you started. Remember to move your vegetables into an ice bath immediately after blanching until they're totally cooled.

Timing and Techniques for Blanching Vegetables

- **Asparagus.** Remove the tough ends from the asparagus. Depending on the storage container, you may need to cut the stems in half. If your stalks are thin, they'll only need 2 minutes of blanching; thick stalks require twice as much.

- **Beans (green or wax).** Remove any tips. Leave the beans whole and blanch them for 3 minutes.

- **Brussels sprouts.** Clean off outer leaves, then soak the sprouts in cold salty water for 30 minutes. Drain and blanch for 4 minutes.

- **Cabbage.** Remove the outer leaves. Shred the cabbage and blanch for just over 1 minute and leave in the water for another 30 seconds before icing.

- **Carrots.** Clean the skins, then slice into ¼ pieces. Blanch for 3 minutes. Whole baby carrots need 5 minutes of blanching.

- **Cauliflower and broccoli.** Break off the pieces from the central core and clean well (a spray nozzle at the sink works very well). Soak in a gallon of salty water (3–4 teaspoons salt) for 30 minutes. Pour off the liquid. Rinse and blanch for 3 minutes.

- **Corn.** Rinse, remove from the cob, and blanch for 5 minutes.
- **Mushrooms (small).** These can be frozen whole. Toss with a little fresh lemon juice and blanch for 4 minutes.
- **Greens (including spinach).** Rinse. Remove any leaves that have spots or other damage. Blanch for 3 minutes.
- **Peas.** Blanch out of the husk for 90 seconds.
- **Peas in the pod.** Trim the ends and remove strings. Blanch for 1–2 minutes, depending on the size of the pod.
- **Peppers.** Slice open and remove the seeds. Cut into the desired size and blanch for 2 minutes.
- **Potatoes.** Wash and scrub thoroughly. Remove the peel and blanch for 4 minutes.
- **Tomatoes.** To easily peel the skins, use a straining spoon and dip the tomatoes in boiling water for 30 seconds. Peel and remove the core. These can be stored whole or diced to desired size.
- **Zucchini and squash.** Peel. Cut into ½-inch slices and blanch for 3 minutes.

Fruit

Do small batches of fruit so it doesn't brown while you're packing. Fruit need not be packed in syrup, but many people do prefer the texture and taste that sugar or sugar syrup adds to frozen fruit. Some folks use sugar substitutes for dietary reasons. In any case, small fruits such as berries take well to a simple sprinkling. Larger chunks such as peaches do well in syrup. The average ratio is ½ cup of syrup to every pint of fruit. Some preservers like to use ascorbic acid to improve the quality of frozen fruit. Adding about ½ teaspoon of this per pint is sufficient; just mix it into the syrup or a little water.

Packaging

Since 95 percent of American homes freeze some of their food regularly, it's not surprising to find people have a lot of questions on the best type of storage containers to use and how to prepare food for the table after it's been frozen. Plastic bags are the most common receptacles, followed by plastic containers. While some people have been known to use glass, this is a bit risky since the glass may crack and break when the food inside expands in the freezing process. Additionally, slippery glass jars coming out of the freezer are easily dropped.

Overall, it's always a good idea to use bags and containers that are rated for freezing. Avoid using waxed cartons; they don't retain the food's quality very well and defrosted food often becomes limp and unstable for handling. Your packaging materials should also be leak and oil resistant, and all packing materials should be able to withstand freezing.

1. **Size Counts**

Another consideration with your containers is size. Think about how many people you plan to serve and choose freezing containers accordingly. If you're going to put several servings in one large container, separate them with a piece of aluminum foil or plastic wrap so you can take out one at a time fairly easily.

2. **Space Constraints**

When you're packing food into a container, always leave a little room for expansion. Let the food reach room temperature before you freeze it (right out of the ice bath is a perfect time with vegetables). Putting warm or hot food in the freezer creates a temperature variance for all the food inside the freezer.

Most importantly, remember to label and date everything. This will help you gauge what should be eaten first so it retains the greatest quality.

3. Wrap It Up

Many preservers wrap the meat with aluminum foil or freezer wrap, then transfer it into another freezer bag or container. This decreases the chance that water crystals will form and protects the foil from being accidentally torn. Note, however, that waxed paper isn't a good choice for freezing because it doesn't resist moisture.

4. Stews and Leftovers

If you know in advance that you'd like to set aside some of what you're cooking for the freezer, it's a good idea to leave it a little undercooked. Freeze the goods as soon as they reach room temperature. When you warm it up, you will finish the cooking process and can also doctor the flavor a bit at that time. Your frozen foods need not be defrosted before you start cooking them. Just remember to get all the packing materials off the item first—you would not be the first person to forget this step and find unpleasant paper or wrapping in a meat serving!

Freezing

Chapter 11: Canning and Preserving Safety Tips

There are a few safety tips that you should follow when you start canning and preserving foods from home. Canning is a great way to store and preserve foods, but it can be risky if not done correctly. However, if you follow these tips, you will be able to can foods in a safe manner.

- **Choose the Right Canner**

The first step to safe home canning is choosing the right canner. First off, know when to use a pressure canner or a water bath canner.

Use a pressure canner that is specifically designed for canning and preserving foods. There are several types of canner out there and some are just for cooking food, not for preserving food and processing jars. Be sure that you have the right type of equipment.

Make sure your pressure canner is the right size. If your canner is too small, the jars may be undercooked. Always opt for a larger canner as the pressure on the bigger pots tends to be more accurate, and you will be able to take advantage of the larger size and can more foods at once! Before you begin canning, check that your pressure canner is in good condition. If your canner has a rubber gasket, it should be flexible and soft. If the rubber is dry or cracked, it should be replaced before you start canning. Be sure your canner is clean and the small vents in the lid are free of debris. Adjust your canner for high altitude processing if needed.

Once you are sure your canner is ready to go and meets all these guidelines, it is time to start canning!

Canning and Preserving Safety Tips

- **Opt for a Screw Top Lid System**

There are many kinds of canning jars that you can choose to purchase. However, the only type of jar that is approved by the USDA is a mason jar with a screw-top lid. These are designated "preserving jars" and are considered the safest and most effective option for home preserving uses.

Some jars are not thought to be safe for home preservation despite being marketed as canning jars. Bail Jars, for example, have a two-part wire clasp lid with a rubber ring in between the lid and jar. While these were popular in the past, it is now thought that the thick rubber and tightly closed lid does not provide a sufficient seal, leading to a higher potential for botulism. Lightening Jars should not be used for canning as they are simply glass jars with glass lids, with no rubber at all. That will not create a good seal!

Reusing jars from store-bought products is another poor idea. They may look like they're in good condition, but they are typically designed to be processed in a commercial facility. Most store-bought products do not have the two-part band and lid system which is best for home canning. Also, the rubber seal on a store-bought product is likely not reusable once you open the original jar. You can reuse store-bought jars at home for storage but not for canning and preserving.

- **Check Your Jars, Lids, and Bands**

As you wash your jars with soapy water, check for any imperfections. Even new jars may have a small chip or crack and need to be discarded. You can reuse jars again and again as long as they are in good condition.

The metal jar rings are also reusable; however, you should only reuse them if they are rust free and undented. If your bands begin to show signs of wear, consider investing in some new ones.

Jar lids need to be new as the sealing compound on the lid can disintegrate over time. When you store your jars in damp places (like in a basement or canning cellar) the lids are even more likely to disintegrate. Always use new lids to ensure that your canning is successful.

- **Check for Recent Canning Updates**

Canning equipment has changed over the years, becoming more high tech and therefore more efficient at processing foods. In addition to the equipment becoming more advanced, there have also been many scientific improvements, making canning safer when the proper steps are taken. For example, many people used to sterilize their jars before pressure canning. While this is still okay to do, it is not necessary as science has shown that any bacteria in the jars will die when heated to such a high temperature in a pressure canner. Sterilization is an extra step that you just don't need!

Make sure that your food preservation information is all up to date and uses current canning guidelines. Avoid outdated cookbooks and reassess "trusted family methods" to make sure they fit into the most recent criteria for safe canning. When in doubt, check with the US Department of Agriculture's Complete Guide to Home Canning which contains the most recent, up-to-date canning tips.

Canning and Preserving Safety Tips

- **Pick the Best Ingredients**

When choosing food to can, always get the best food possible. You want to use high quality, perfectly ripe produce for canning. You will never end up with a jar of food better than the product itself, so picking good ingredients is important to the taste of your final product. Also, products that past its prime can affect the ability to can it. If strawberries are overripe, your jam may come out too runny. If your tomatoes are past their prime, they may not have a high enough pH level to be processed in a water bath. Pick your ingredients well and you will make successful preserved foods.

- **Clean Everything**

While you may know that your jars and lids need to be washed and sanitized, don't forget about the rest of your tools. Cleaning out your canner before using it is essential, even if you put it away clean. Make sure to wipe your countertop well, making sure there are no crumbs or residue. Wash your produce with clean, cold water and don't forget to wash your hands! The cleaner everything is, the less likely you are to spread bacteria onto your jarred foods

- **Follow Your Recipe**

Use recipes from trusted sources and be sure to follow them to the letter. Changing the amount of one or two ingredients may alter the balance of acidity and could result in unsafe canning (especially when using a water bath canner). Use the ingredients as directed and make very few changes—none if possible.

Adhere to the processing times specified by your recipe. Sometimes the times may seem a little long, but the long processing time is what makes these products safe to store on the shelf. The processing time is the correct amount of time needed to destroy spoilage organisms, mold spores, yeast and pathogens in the jar. So, as you may have guessed, it is extremely important to use the times that are written in your recipe as a hard rule.

- **Cool the Jars**

Be sure that you give your jars 12 hours to cool before testing the seal. If you test the seal too early, it may break as the jar is still warm, making the rubber pliable. Be sure to cool the jars away from a window or fan as even a slight breeze may cause the hot jars to crack. Once cool, remove the metal band, clean it and save it for your next canning project.

- **Don't Risk It**

If you suspect that the food you have canned is bad, don't try to eat it, just toss it! Each time you open a jar of canned food, inspect it and check for the following:

1. Is the lid bulging, swollen, or leaking at all?
2. If the jar cracked or damaged?
3. Does the jar foam when opened?
4. Is the food inside discolored or moldy?
5. Does the food smell bad?

If you notice any of these warning signs in a food that you have canned, throw it away. Do not taste it to check if it is good. It is not worth risking your health to try the food after seeing one of the above signs.

Canning and Preserving Safety Tips

Luckily, it is fairly easy to spot a jar of food that has gone bad. Home-canned food can spoil for many reasons. A dent in the lid, a small crack in the jar, an improper seal, or not enough processing time are all common errors that may cause canned foods to go bad. Follow the exact canning directions and hopefully, you will never get a bad jar of food!

Canning and Preserving Safety Tips

Chapter 12: Canning Do's and Don'ts

Canning is relatively simple but when not done properly, it can result in disastrous consequences. For you to truly be a master on this very important skill, let me provide you with some canning dos and don'ts that you'll surely find helpful.

1. Be Organized

Did you notice that in both water bath and pressure canning methods above studying the recipe is always the first step? This is because knowing what to do keeps you organized. You have to be organized when preserving food since it could help your work go smoothly and canning should be done as quickly as possible.

2. Spices and seasoning only as specified

Do you know that spices and seasoning are usually high in bacteria? Having too many seasonings and spices on your food beyond what was required in the recipe could be unsafe.

3. Overripe fruits and vegetables are a no-no

I have mentioned this before but let me just reiterate this for you, canning can increase the life of the food but it certainly couldn't increase its quality. Canning overripe fruits may become worse in storage.

4. No butter and fat ever

You should not put these two in your home canned products as they do not store well. Adding them to your product will only decrease the food's life. In addition, butter and fat slows heat transfer during the processing time which can result to an unsafe preserve.

5. **You can go smaller but not bigger**

When it comes to the size of jar you should use, if you can't stick to the jar size on the recipe, then you should pick up a smaller jar than getting a bigger one since this can result in an unsafe product.

6. **The higher the altitude = longer processing time**

In high altitudes, the boiling point is of lower altitude. This is why you have to increase the processing time to compensate for the lower temperatures at an altitude above 1000 feet.

7. **Hot and cold do not go well together**

Indeed, hot and cold do not go well together especially when it comes to jars. Abrupt changes in temperature would certainly result in breakage so here are things you should remember: if the food will be hot when placed in the jar, your jar should be preheated and the water in the canner should already be heated to. If the food is cold, do not preheat the jars, just sterilize them. Also, put the jars before turning on the heat on the canner so that the water and the food can be heated together.

8. **Safety first before removing jars**

After the processing time, jars will sure to be hot in both the water bath and the pressure canning method so you have to make sure to handle them carefully. You can use a footstool to avoid tiptoeing while removing the jars because that could be dangerous!

9. **Patience on seals**

After removing the jars from the rack and putting them on a paper towel, avoid moving them or you will be interrupting its sealing process. Just leave them be or else put the jars in a place where it wouldn't be disturbed the moment you take them out of the canner.

Canning Do's and Don'ts

10. Write the details down meticulously

I'm just talking about the labels on the jars. Remember to always attach a label to each jar and write down the recipe and the production date. This is the best way to keep track of the life span of the food.

To be truly a master of something, you have to work hard on it too. Knowledge of the steps in canning and preserving plus the additional tips I mentioned would not be enough to create a canning master in you. You have to work hard on it too. As always, practice is the key!

Canning Do's and Don'ts

Chapter 13: Some Other Food Preservation Techniques

The Milling Technique

The ancient humans found out that by crushing different berries and wheat kernels by placing them in between two pieces of rocks they can get flour, which can be used in a variety of different forms. Since that time grinding flour with the help of various techniques has been part of human civilization.

Milling is used as the easiest way of getting the fullest nutrient content from wheat flour. This method is the demand for modern day as the shelf life of flour needs to be increased as food is supplied from one part of the world to the other. For this reason, the removal of all sorts of grain bran traces and germs is highly essential. Milling as a procedure will enable the user to get the required amount of flour every time so that it can be consumed within a time period of 72 hours.

- **Why go for milling:**

The flour grains consist of around 90% of minerals, vitamins, and protein which are needed by the human body. But in the case of commercially milled flour, the quantity of these nutrients is largely reduced because of artificial additives and processing.

The whole grain comprises of three major parts, two being the germ and the bran. These two hold all of the minerals, vitamins, and proteins. On the other hand, when milled, the oils present in the germ and bran starts oxidizing. So eventually, the flour turns rancid within a period of 72 hours. So the commercial packaging of flour removes all bran and of germ and thus all the connected nutrients, which elongates the shelf life. In Commercially processed flour you will get only the third ingredient of the grain, called endosperm. It is the starchy center, which is white in color and no useful nutrients are present in it.

Methods Applied

If you are also curious about the quality of food you eat and especially the most frequently used eatable, i.e. flour. You need to be curious about this method of food processing.

Various methods of milling are applied, some of which include:

- **Manual Milling**

This allows manual milling of Grain, in which a mill that is operated by hand is applied. Although time-consuming yet this method is quite cost-friendly.

- **Electric Milling**

As compared to manual method electric milling is fast in which mill is supplied with a power connection. If you have to mill large quantities of flour, then this method is the most suitable one.

- **Motorized Milling**

Flour can also be milled in a way that is partially supported by the machines. In this method, the mill is connected to an electric or gas motor along with a pulley system. This method is faster than manual milling but slower than the electric milling process.

The equipment used for various types of mills is as follows:

Some Other Food Preservation Techniques

1. In the case of the stone mill is a set of two grinding stones that are circular in shape. One stein is kept stationary while the other one is moved against it.
2. In the case of burr mill, the grinding wheels of the wheel are made up of steel with tiny burrs extending from the sides.
3. In the case of impact mill, the major assembly is just like the stone mill but various rows of blades are used to circular rows.

Some Other Food Preservation Techniques

Chapter 14: FAQ'S On Canning & Preserving Foods

This book has tried to cover all areas that a beginner or newbie in canning and preserving food would want to know. Nevertheless, there may still be some questions that are hanging in your mind. Here are the most frequently asked questions and their answers regarding canning and preserving foods.

As an interested beginner who would like to take this skill into a higher level, is there a canning class or course that one can take?
Anybody can preserve or can foods without formal education. For those who would like to have advanced canning skills, canning classes are oftentimes offered in some grocery stores, kitchen stores, cooking schools, community centers, and sometimes, even in libraries. You could also search online for correspondence that offers this course. Be careful with blogs or articles that teach canning techniques. Some of these articles may contain ideas or suggestions that go contrary to the recommendations of USDA. If in doubt, refer to the USDA manual or contact an authorized person.

What is the shelf life of canned food?
Properly sealed canned and preserved foods placed in a cool, dry place, with no signs of spoilage inside and out, are considered safe to consume for at least a year. However, canned foods stored near a furnace, in indirect sunlight, a range or anywhere warm can decrease

shelf life. It would be safe to consume within a few weeks until a couple of months only. Placing the jars or cans in damp areas may corrode cans and this can cause leakage, causing the food to be contaminated and unsafe to eat.

One of the recipes included pectin as an ingredient in making jams. If a person does not like to use pectin, can he or she omit that ingredient?

Emphasis on the importance of complying with the recipes has been stressed over and over again throughout this book. Do not modify, lessen, remove, or add anything to the recipe if you want to have a perfect outcome. There are many reliable recipes that you can find that do not use pectin. Use these instead rather than trying to change the recipe.

Can you process two layers of jars at one time?

Yes, this can be done. The jars at the upper layer would enjoy the same benefits as those in the bottom. The temperature is equally distributed making it safe for all jars, whether in the upper and lower layer. Just make sure that you place a wire rack between the layers to allow the circulation of water and steam around the jars. Also, when using bath-water canning method, make sure that the water is up to one inch above the tops of the jars in the upper layer. If you are using a pressure canner, the water should be 2 to 3 inches from the bottom. As always, comply with the processing time and required temperature.

During processing, some liquid of the contents were lost. What should be done about it?

If the liquid loss is minimal, there is nothing to worry about. The food will not spoil and the seal will not be affected. It may cause slight discoloration of the food, however, but that's about it. However, if the liquid loss is at least half of the original amount, then the most that you can do is to refrigerate it and consume within 2 to 3 days.

What is kettle canning and is this safe to use?

In this method, the foods to be preserved are cooked in an ordinary household kettle. After that, the foods are placed into hot jars, covered, and sealed. You would notice that no processing is done in this method. In addition, the temperature when using the kettle canning method is not high enough to eliminate the harmful bacteria that may be in the food. Also, during the transfer of food from the kettle to the jars, microorganisms can enter the food and cause spoilage and worse, food poisoning, later on. Therefore, the safety of food is not guaranteed. The kettle canning method is not included in the recommendation of USDA with regards to canning.

Why do some jars break during canning?

There are many reasons breakage occurs during the process of canning. Here are five reasons:

1. The glass of the jar is not tempered. A tempered or toughened glass underwent a process that increased its strength and ability to withstand heat compared to normal glass. Before buying commercial food jars,

2. Another reason is using jars with hairline cracks. These cracks are so thin that they can be missed or overlooked. Such jars would not be able to stand the extreme heat during processing time.
3. Not placing a wire rack on the bottom of the pot or canner could also cause the jars to break.
4. Putting newly cooked food into cold jars. The difference in the temperature between the food and the jars could lead to breakage. That is why it is advised that the jars should be maintained on a hot temperature before filling them with hot food.
5. Jars with unheated or raw food placed directly into boiling water can also break because of the sudden change in temperature. It is better to use hot water first and let it achieve boiling point after several minutes.

An article said that a jam or jelly with molds could still be used. Simply remove or scoop out the parts with molds. The rest would still be okay for consumption. Is this true?

Molds can cause an increase in the pH of the food. For instance, if the canned food is high acid, then because of the raised pH, it could become low acid. This places the preserved food into the risk of having botulism and other bacterial growth. Therefore, all canned foods with molds should be disposed of properly. Follow the proper waste disposal for spoiled canned food.

Can canning be done for those people with special diets?

Some people, because of their medical conditions, would not be allowed to consume some of the canned foods because of some ingredients like sugar and salt. Sugar is discouraged among Diabetic people due to the effect of increased blood sugar with the intake of simple sugar.

On the other hand, salts are always restricted among people with cardiovascular disorders as this can cause increased high blood pressure as more body water is retained because of salts. Still, canning foods can be done for these people even in the absence of salt or sugar. However, the color, texture, flavor of these canned foods will differ from those with sugar or salt in them, as expected. Other people find these special diet canned foods to be less acceptable and less appealing.

You can preserve and can regular fruits even without sugar. The key is selecting firm, fully ripe (but not overripe) fruits of the best quality. In place of sugar syrup, you can use unsweetened fruit juice or plain water. Another technique is to blend some of the same fruits to be canned. This will serve as the syrup or juice of the canned food. Pour the blended fruits into the jar and then add the solid fruits. To make this more palatable, you can add sugar substitutes when serving.

To can vegetables, meats, seafood, or tomatoes without salt, proceed with the regular canning minus the salt. This method is allowed, as salts are not considered as preservatives, hence the safety of food is still guaranteed even in the absence of salt. Salt substitutes can be offered upon serving to make the preserved food taste better.

What is the future of canning and preserving foods?

The trend all over the world right now is towards healthy food and lifestyle. You can see everything "organic" from cosmetics, hair products, food, baby products, and even processed foods. People prefer "fresh" than canned or commercially prepared processed foods.

This is where home canning and preserving fresh fruits, meats, poultry, salsa, vegetables, sauces, and what-have-you enter the picture. This is a combination of being healthy and modern, rolled into one. It meets the requirements of being healthy and at the same time, lasting longer on the shelf or pantry. It is ready to eat, answering the need for convenience and saving precious time.

More and more people are going into canning and preserving food. The threat of not having enough good food to eat in the future due to excessive wasting and unnecessary throwing of food today has found its solution in canning.

Final words on canning and preserving foods

Canning is not only easy, fun, profitable, helpful (both physically and financially) but it is also Earth-friendly. This generation has been blessed with abundance in everything, most especially in the production of food. That is no excuse to be unwise and thoughtless. Make use of excess resources and learn how to preserve and prolong their life spans, rather than just throw them away. Can and preserve food today. This is a good thing to do.

Conclusion

After reading all of this you might be feeling a little overwhelmed. Don't panic, this is natural. Do not let a large amount of information phase you. This book was not written to scare you or make you feel incompetent. No. If anything, this book was written to help you navigate through the challenges home canning may throw in your direction.

Canning your own food is a deeply satisfying activity. When you take a look at your canned foods and you realize that you were able to do it on your own, it will fuel the motivation you need to turn this into a regular habit. If you choose to can your own food on a regular basis, you will notice a decline in the amount of money you use to buy produce and other canned foods. Home canning will also influence your eating habits in a positive way. The foods you will be preserved will be far healthier than the preserved foods that are sold in supermarkets.

Once you get the hang of canning your own food, you will be unstoppable! I will not lie to you and tell you that everything will be easy – especially the first couple of times. You will make a couple of mistakes and you might make a mess of your kitchen too. This is expected – you are a beginner after all.

As time goes by, though, the number of mistakes you make will decrease, and eventually, you won't need this guide to assist you. You will be able to come up with creative recipes of your own! This all has

Conclusion

to start with the first steps, the first steps being you arr giving this a chance.

If you aren't feeling confident in your abilities, try out the easiest water bath canning recipe in this book. You can also find a number of safe and USDA approved recipes online. There are a number of forums dedicated to offering support to home canning beginners.

Don't let your fears stop you from trying out this great method of preserving your own food. It is a highly rewarding experience that is capable of benefitting you for years to come.

You won't regret trying it out.

Thank you again for downloading this book!

I hope this book was able to help you know the basics of food canning and preservation. I hope that this book was able to clearly explain the different concepts and rules when it comes to canning and preserving food. I also hope that you'll be able to follow all the instructions indicated in this book.

The next step is to apply all the things that you have learned from this book. Remember that knowledge without application is useless. Look for canning and preservation recipes online or from different books and start doing them yourself. Just see to it that you will always take into consideration the reminders, especially the fact that you first have to understand the method that you are going to carry out before you start doing anything.

Made in the USA
Middletown, DE
23 July 2020